hide this mandarin chinese phrase book

Hide This Mandarin Chinese Phrase Book

Contacting the Editors
Every effort has been made to provide accurate information in this publication, but changes are inevitable. The publisher cannot be responsible for any resulting loss, inconvenience or injury. We would appreciate it if readers would call our attention to any errors or outdated information by contacting APA Publications GmbH & Co. Verlag KG. 38 Joo Koon Road, Singapore 628990. email: apasin@singnet.com.sg

First Printing: September 2008
Printed in Singapore

Translation, Adaptation and Interior Layout: Lingua Tech (S) Pte Ltd
Editor/Project Manager: Susan Chan
Cover Layout: Pann Wong
Illustrations: Kyle Webster, Amy Zaleski; Gin Tan

INSIDE

INTRO

So, you're going to a Chinese-speaking country, huh? Well then, you'd better learn a couple of useful phrases. By "useful" we mean the lingo you need to hook up, check in, and hang out. This un-censored phrase book's got you covered with everything you need to speak cool Chinese—saying hi, getting a room, spending your bucks, finding a cheap place to eat, scoring digits... and a helluva lot more. We've even thrown in a few totally offensive, completely inappropriate, and downright nasty terms—just for fun. You'll be able to easily spot these by looking for .

We've got your back with insider tips, too. Check these out for up-to-date info that'll help you maneuver around a Chinese locale...

cool facts that may seem like fiction

tips on what's hot and what's not

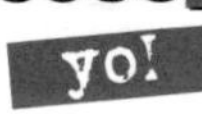

info you've gotta know

Warning —this language can get you into trouble. If you wanna say it in public, that's up to you. But we're not taking the rap (like responsibility and liability) for any problems you could encounter by using the expressions in this book. These include, but are not limited to, verbal and/or physical abuse, bar brawls, cat fights, arrest... Use caution when dealing with Chinese that's hot!

SPEAK CHINESE - THE EASY WAY

This book will not make you an expert in Chinese, but it will help you get through your stay without sounding like a loser when speaking the language. To make it easy for you, we've provided really simple phonetics (those letters right under the Chinese expressions) with every entry you could say out loud. Just take note that not all pinyin* letters or letter combinations are pronounced as they normally are in English. We've prepared a quick guide to the pinyin system to help you. (*Pinyin is the most widely used romanization and pronunciation system for Chinese.)

Initial Consonants

Here are the initial sounds in pinyin, and their equivalents in English.

Letters	Approximate Pronunciation	Example	Pronunciation
c	like ts in pits	草	cǎo
ch	like ch in church	吃	chī
h	like ch in the Scottish loch	花	huā
q	like ch in chip	旗	qí
r	like r in raw	人	rén
sh	like sh in wash, with the tongue curved at the back of the mouth	是	shì
x	like sh in she, with the tongue resting at the back of the lower teeth	心	xīn
z	like ds in kids	子	zǐ
zh	like j in judge	中	zhōng

The letters b,d,f,g,j,k,l,m,n,p,s,t,w are pronounced generally as in English.

Finals

Here are the final sounds in pinyin, and their equivalents in English.

Symbol	Approximate Pronunciation	Example	Pronunciation
a	like a in father	八	bā
e	like e in her	鹅	é
i	1. like e in me 2. not pronounced after c,s,z 3. after ch,sh,zh,and r,pronounce all letters of the syllable with the tongue curled back, like I in bird	1. 一 2. 此 3. 吃	1. yī 2. cǐ 3. chī
o	like aw in awe	我	wǒ
u	like oo in spoon	五	wǔ
ü	like pronouncing you with lips pursed	女	nǚ
ai	like ai in aisle	爱	ài
an	like an in ran	安	ān
ang	like ang in rang	昂	áng
ao	like ow in how	奥	ào
ei	like ei in eight	类	lèi
en	like en in open	恩	ēn
eng	like en in open + g	衡	héng
er	like err, but with tongue curled back and the sound coming from the back of the throat	二	èr
ia	like ya in yard	下	xià
ian	similar to yen	联	lián
iang	like ee-ang	两	liǎng
iao	like ee-ow	料	liào
ie	like ye in yes	列	liè
in	like in in thin	林	lín
ing	like ing in thing	龄	líng

iong	like ee-ong	雄	xióng
iu	like yo in yoga	六	liù
ou	like ou in dough	楼	lóu
ong	like oong with oo as in soon	龙	lóng
ua	like wah	华	huá
uai	similar to why	怀	huái
uan	like wahn	环	huán
uang	like wahng	黄	huáng
ue	like u+ eh	学	xué
ui	similar to way	会	huì
un	like uan in truant	魂	hún
uo	similar to war	或	huò

The Four Tones

Tone	Mark	Description	Example	Simplified Chinese	Translation
1st	¯	high and level	mā	妈	mother
2nd	´	starts medium in tone, then rises to the top	má	麻	hemp
3rd	˘	starts low at the level 2, dips to the bottom and then rises toward the top to level 4	mă	马	horse
4th	`	starts at the top and then falls sharp and strong to the bottom	mà	骂	scold
Vowels without tonal marks are considered "neutral" or the fifth tone:					
neutral		flat, with no emphasis	ma		an expression of mood

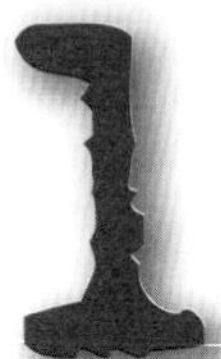

THE BASICS

hi there

Make a good impression on the locals from the get-go.

Hello!	你好！ *nǐ hǎo* Formal yet friendly.
Hi!	嗨！ *hài* Casual and to the point.
Hi, how are you?	嗨，你好！ *hài, nǐ hǎo*
Good evening.	晚上好。 *wǎn shàng hǎo*

how're you doin'?

Ask about someone's well-being.

How are you?	你好！ *nǐ hǎo*
What's up?	你好吗? *nǐ hǎo ma*
How's it going?	最近怎么样? *zuì jìn zěn me yàng*
Doing well?	一切都好吗? *yì qiè dōu hǎo ma*

the scoop

When meeting someone for the first time, the Chinese usually say 你好 (nǐ hǎo). This is often done simultaneously with or followed closely by a handshake. Handshakes should be firm to show your sincerity. Despite great modernization taking place throughout the nation, the Chinese are basically pretty conservative in their show of affection. It's best to avoid hugs and air kisses when you meet someone for the first time – unless you are fond of shocking your host(s)!

hey you!

Wanna get someone's attention? Try these.

Excuse me!	嗨! *hài* *Not to be used as an apology.*
Sir! / Ma'am!	先生! / 夫人! *xiān shēng / fū rén* *Use this when you wanna be polite.*
Yo!	唷! *yòu* *A quick way to get someone's attention.*
Hey!	嘿! *hèi*

FACT In formal situations, use 先生 (xiān shēng) for men, 女士 (nǚ shì) for women, and 小姐 (xiáo jǐe) for young ladies. For example, Zhāng xiān shēng (Mr. Zhāng), Zhāng nǚ shì (Mrs. Zhāng or Ms. Zhāng), or Zhāng xiáo jǐe (Miss Zhāng). If you're with close friends, you may address an older person as Lǎo (老) Zhāng (if his or her last name is Zhāng). Someone who is your peer or younger is xiáo (小) Zhāng. A word of caution: only do this if you are really close friends!

sorry

Oops…need to apologize?

My bad.	我的错。 *wǒ de cuò*
Excuse me!	不好意思! *bù hǎo yì si*
Sorry!	对不起! *duì bù qǐ*
I'm sorry.	对不起! *duì bù qǐ*
I'm truly very sorry.	真的非常对不起。 *zhēn de fēi cháng duì bù qǐ*
I was bad.	都是我的错。 *dōu shì wǒ de cuò*
I didn't mean to do that.	我不是故意的。 *wǒ bú shì gù yì de*

huh?

What did he or she just say? Make sure you understand it correctly.

Do you speak English?	你会说英语吗? *nǐ huì shuō yīng yǔ ma* *It's OK to ask if he or she speaks English.*
What was that?	你说什么? *nǐ shuō shén me*
Could you spell it?	可以拼写出来吗? *ké yǐ pīn xiě chū lái ma*
Please write it down.	请写下来。 *qǐng xiě xià lái*
Can you translate this for me?	可以为我翻译一下吗? *ké yǐ wéi wǒ fān yì yí xià ma*
I (don't) understand.	我（不）明白。 *wǒ (bù) míng bai*
Do you understand?	你明白吗? *nǐ míng bai ma* *Let's hope someone has a clue as to what's going on!*
Can you repeat that?	可以重复一遍吗? *ké yǐ chóng fù yí biàn ma*
Can you repeat slowly?	可以慢点重复一遍吗? *ké yǐ màn diǎn chóng fù yí biàn ma*

help

Got yourself into a sticky situation?

Can you help me?	你能帮我一下吗? *nǐ néng bāng wǒ yí xià ma*
Help!	救命啊! *jiù mìng ā*
Call the police!	快报警! *kuài bào jǐng*
Stop thief!	拦住小偷! *lán zhù xiǎo tōu*
Fire!	着火了! *zháo huǒ le*
I'm lost.	我迷路了。 *wǒ mí lù le*
Get a doctor!	赶紧找个医生! *gán jǐn zhǎo gè yī sheng*

emergency

Just in case you get into trouble.

Where's the nearest police station?	请问最近的警察局在哪儿? *qǐng wèn zuì jìn de jǐng chá jú zài nǎ ér*

In an emergency, dial 110 for the police; 120 for the ambulance; and 119 for the fire department.

I want to report ...	我要报告... *wǒ yào bào gào...*
an accident.	事故。 *shì gù*
an attack.	攻击。 *gōng jī*
a mugging.	抢劫。 *qiǎng jié*
a rape.	强奸。 *qiáng jiān*
a theft.	偷窃。 *tōu qiè*
I've been robbed.	我被打劫了。 *wǒ bèi dǎ jié le*
I've been mugged.	我被打抢了。 *wǒ bèi dǎ qiǎng le*
I need to contact the consulate.	我要联系一下领事馆。 *wǒ yào lián xì yí xià lǐng shì guǎn*

bye-bye

From classic to cool, here are the best ways to say good-bye.

Good-bye.	再见。 *zài jiàn*
Bye!	再会! *zài huì*
See you later.	回头见。 *huí tóu jiàn*

See you soon. 回见。
huí jiàn

Good night. 晚安。
wǎn ān
Say it only when it's bedtime.

thank you!

Show someone your appreciation and gratitude.

Thank you! 谢谢！
xiè xiè

Thank you for your help! 谢谢你帮忙！
xiè xiè nǐ bāng máng

Thank you very much indeed. 真的非常感谢你！
zhēn de fēi cháng gǎn xiè nǐ

I'm really grateful for your help. 非常感谢你帮忙！
fēi cháng gǎn xiè nǐ bāng máng

2 GETTIN' AROUND

by plane

Just arrived? Going somewhere? Act like you know what you're doing.

To ..., please.	请给我一张到....的机票。 *qǐng gěi wǒ yì zhāng dào ... de jī piào*
One-way. / Round-trip.	单程。/ 往返。 *dān chéng / wáng fǎn*
How much?	请问多少钱? *qǐng wèn duō shǎo qián* Quick and to the point.
Are there any discounts?	请问有没有折扣? *qǐng wèn yǒu méi yǒu zhé kòu* Doesn't hurt to ask!
When is the (...) flight to ...?	请问到 ... 的 (...) 航班几点钟? *qǐng wèn dào ... de (...) háng bān jǐ diǎn zhōng*
(first)	首个 *shǒu gè*
(next)	下一个 *xià yí gè*
(last)	最后一个 *zuì hòu yí gè*
I'd like ... ticket(s).	我想要...票。 *wǒ xiǎng yào ... piào*
one	一张 *yì zhāng*
two	两张 *liǎng zhāng*

Is there any delay on flight …?	请问航班…晚点了吗? *qǐng wèn háng bān … wán diǎn le ma*
How late will it be?	晚点多久? *wán diǎn duō jiǔ*
Which gate does flight … leave from?	请问航班…的登机门是哪个? *qǐng wèn háng bān … de dēng jī mén shì nǎ gè*
Where is / are …?	…在哪儿? *… zài nǎ ér*
the baggage check	行李检查处 *xíng li jiǎn chá chǔ*
the luggage carts	行李托运处 *xíng li tuō yùn chù*

the scoop

Need cheap airline tickets? China's many domestic airlines offer great deals throughout the year. Most international flights bring you directly to Beijing, Shanghai or Hongkong, and from there, you can connect to almost all other cities via domestic flights. Do your research online or check with the many air-ticketing agencies in the three cities. Compare prices to ensure that you get the best deal.

There are three major nation-wide holidays in China: the Spring holiday (usually sometime between mid Jan and mid Feb), the May Day holiday (1st of May), and the National Day holiday (1st of October). Each of these holidays lasts for about seven days at a stretch. If you plan to go sightseeing, you'd really want to avoid these periods when half the country is either on holiday (with you!) or jostling for air- and train-tickets (with you!).

in flight

Sit back (if possible) and enjoy.

Can I have a blanket / pillow?	请问能给我一张毯子 / 一个枕头? *qǐng wèn néng gěi wǒ yì zhāng tǎn zi / yí gè zhěn tou*
I ordered a … meal	我订了一份…餐饮。 *wǒ dìng le yí fèn … cān yǐn*
diabetic	适合糖尿病人的 *shì hé táng niào bìng rén de*
gluten free	没有麸质的 *méi yǒu fū zhì de*
kosher	犹太教的洁食 *yóu tài jiāo de jié shí*
low calorie / low cholesterol/ low fat / low sodium	低热量 / 低胆固醇 / 低脂肪 / 低钠的 *dī rè liàng / dī dǎn gù chún / dī zhī fáng / dī nà de*
vegetarian	素食 *sù shí*
I need a barf bag.	我需要一个呕吐袋。 *wǒ xū yào yí gè ǒu tù dài* Gross.

your stuff

Find it, grab it, and go!

Where is the luggage from flight …?	…航班的行李在哪儿? *… háng bān de xíng li zài nǎ ér*

My luggage has been stolen.	我的行李被偷了。 *wǒ de xíng li bèi tōu le*
My suitcase was damaged.	我的手提箱被弄坏了。 *wǒ de shǒu tí xiāng bèi nòng huài le*
Our luggage hasn't arrived.	我们的行李还没到。 *wǒ men de xíng li hái méi dào* What a nightmare.

Just arrived in China? There are many ways to get from the airport to your hotel. In Beijing, Shanghai, and other major cities, you can take the airport shuttle buses. (Each passenger pays around 20-30 RMB.) These buses operate on a fixed route, and you will be dropped off at major hotels or at a spot near your hotel.

Alternatively, you could take a taxi, which might cost between 80-150 RMB, depending on where you're going. Most taxi drivers do not speak English so it would be handy to have the destination address in Chinese. Remember to get a receipt from the taxi driver – just in case you leave anything behind, the receipt will enable the local authorities to locate the driver. In Shanghai, the new Maglev Monorail, capable of running at a top speed of over 310 mph, can bring you from the Pudong International Airport to the Lujiazui financial district (30 km away) in just 8 minutes! Tickets cost about 50 RMB per person. (Passengers with air-tickets in hand pay 40 RMB.) A must-try!

First-time visitors to Beijing will want to check these world-famous venues off their list: the Great Wall, the Forbidden City, the Summer Palace, the Temple of Heaven, the Tiananmen Square, and the fast disappearing Beijing hú-tòng (traditional alleys). In Shanghai, there's the Bund, the French Concession area, the People's Square, Yuyuan, and the Water Towns of Jiangnan. These days, those with an appetite for adventure head north to Inner Mongolia, venture south to Xinjiang, or go west to Tibet and the Silk Road.

by train

OK, first, you gotta get there.

How do I get to the (main) train station?	请问火车站（总站）怎么走? *qǐng wèn huǒ chē zhàn (zǒng zhàn) zěn me zǒu*
Is it far?	远吗? *yuǎn ma*

waitin' for the train

Learn to negotiate your way around the station.

Where is / are ...?	请问...在哪? *qǐng wèn ... zài nǎ*
the bathroom	厕所 *cè suǒ*
the currency exchange office	钱币兑换处 *qián bì duì huàn chù*

the baggage check 行李检查处
xíng li jiăn chá chŭ

the lost-and-found 失物招领处
shī wù zhāo lĭng chù

the luggage lockers 行李寄存处
xíng li jì cún chù

the platforms 站台
zhàn tái

the snack bar 小卖部
xiăo mài bù

Where is / are …? 请问...在哪?
qĭng wèn ... zài nă

the ticket office 售票处
shòu piào chù

the waiting room 候车室
hòu chē shì

Where can I buy a ticket? 请问售票处在哪?
qĭng wèn shòu piào chù zài nă

I'd like a (…) ticket to … 我想要到 ... 的 (...) 票。
wŏ xiăng yào dào ... de (...) piào

(one-way) 单程
dān chéng

(round-trip) 往返
wáng făn

How much is that? 请问多少钱?
qĭng wèn duō shăo qián

Is there a discount for students? 请问学生有折扣吗?
qĭng wèn xué sheng yŏu zhé kòu ma

Do you offer a cheap same day round-trip ticket? 请问有没有当天往返的廉价机票?
qǐng wèn yǒu méi yǒu dàng tiān wáng fǎn de lián jià jī piào

Could I have a schedule? 您可以给我一张时刻表吗?
nín ké yǐ gěi wǒ yì zhāng shí kè biǎo ma

How long is the trip? 请问多久能到?
qǐng wèn duō jiǔ néng dào

When is the (...) train to ...? 到 ... 的 (...) 列车是几点?
dào ... de (...) liè chē shì jǐ diǎn

(first) 第一趟
dì yí tàng

(next) 下一趟
xià yí tàng

(last) 最后一趟
zuì hòu yí tàng

train talk

Whether you're waiting for the train or looking for a seat, make conversation with a good-looking Chinese guy or girl.

Hello. Where is platform ...? 你好，站台...在哪?
nǐ hǎo, zhàn tái ... zài nǎ

Is this the train to ...? 这是到...的列车吗?
zhè shì dào ... de liè chē ma
I bet you're hoping he/she will be on your train.

Is this seat taken? 这个座位有人吗?
zhè ge zuò wèi yǒu rén ma
It may be a long ride—find someone to enjoy it with.

Do you mind if I sit here? 我可以坐这儿吗?
wǒ ké yǐ zuò zhè ér ma
Get a little closer.

the scoop

You can't go wrong with trains in China. Trains are such a vital mode of transport, there's a full ministry (the Ministry of Railways) overseeing the country's massive train network and operations.

There are four classes of tickets: hard seats, soft seats, hard sleepers, and soft sleepers. Tickets can be purchased from train stations, ticketing agencies throughout the cities, and possibly even from your hotel.

It is quite common for larger cities like Beijing and Shanghai to have more than one train station. So make sure you confirm your departure and arrival station if you are traveling by train.

During the major holidays, train tickets sell out very quickly as millions of Chinese in the cities travel to their vacation destinations, or home towns for family visits. Book your train tickets way ahead in advance if you are planning to travel during these periods.

by bus

It's not always the fastest way to get around, but it sure beats walking!

Where is the bus station?	请问车站在哪? *qǐng wèn chē zhàn zài nǎ*
Where can I buy tickets?	请问售票处在哪? *qǐng wèn shòu piào chù zài nǎ*
A one-way / round-trip ticket to …	请给我一张到...的单程 / 往返车票 *qǐng gěi wǒ yì zhāng dào … de dān chéng / wáng fǎn chē piào*
How much is the fare to …?	到...的车费多少? *dào … de chē fèi duō shǎo*
Is this the right bus to …?	这是到...的车吗? *zhè shì dào … de chē ma*
Could you tell me when to get off?	该下车的时候能告诉我一声吗? *gāi xià chē de shí hou néng gào su wǒ yì shēng ma* Just in case you have no clue as to where you're headed...
Next stop, please!	下一站停车，谢谢! *xià yí zhàn tíng chē， xiè xiè* If you want the driver to stop, better say please!

by subway

Is goin' underground your style? Then you'll need these.

Where's the nearest subway station?	请问最近的地铁站在哪? *qǐng wèn zuì jìn de dì tiě zhàn zài nǎ* *Please let it be in walking distance.*
Where can I buy a ticket?	请问售票处在哪? *qǐng wèn shòu piào chù zài nǎ*
Could I have a map of the subway?	请问能给我一份地铁的地图吗? *qǐng wèn néng gěi wǒ yí fèn dì tiě de dì tú ma* *If you ask nicely, you may actually get what you want.*
Which line should I take for …?	请问到...应坐哪条线? *qǐng wèn dào … yīng zuò nǎ tiáo xiàn* *If the subway map is incomprehensible, ask a cutie for help.*
Is the next stop …?	下一站是...吗? *xià yí zhàn shì … ma*
Where are we?	我们到哪一站了? *wǒ men dào nǎ yí zhàn le* *Don't have a clue, huh?!*

If getting trapped in big city traffic jams is not your cup of tea, give the subway a try. It is an inexpensive, and possibly faster alternative. Train networks usually cover the central downtown area and connect the more prominent landmarks or locations. However, trains can get extremely crowded during the morning and evening peak hours. Get ready to brave the crush of the rush hour! Fares range from 3-6 RMB and trains normally operate from around 5am to midnight.

by taxi

Feelin' lazy? Get a cab.

Where can I get a taxi?	请问在哪可以搭到计程车? *qǐng wèn zài nǎ ké yǐ dā dào jì chéng chē*
Please take me to …	请带我去... *qǐng dài wǒ qù …*
a good bar.	一家不错的酒吧 *yì jiā bú cuò de jiǔ bā*
a good club.	一家不错的俱乐部 *yì jiā bú cuò de jù lè bù*
the airport.	机场 *jī chǎng*
the train station.	火车站 *huǒ chē zhàn*
this address.	这个地址 *zhè ge dì zhǐ*

How much is that? 多少钱?
duō shǎo qián

Keep the change. 不用找了。
bú yòng zhǎo le

Most taxis in China are metered. Look for the 出租 (chū zū) sign on top of the taxi. The charges vary from city to city. (The flag down fee ranges from 5-12 RMB and the rate is normally about 2-3 RMB per mile.) Taxi trips can cost a lot more during rush hour as taxis get stuck in traffic jams for ages. So avoid the rush hour if you can.

Most taxi drivers do not speak English. Have the name and location of your destination written in Chinese – if you can – to avoid confusion. At the hotel, airport, train station, etc, wait at the taxi line, and get a taxi from an authorized taxi company. If someone tries to bring you to his own taxi, say "No" as these taxis are illegal and you may end up paying much more than you should. Some of these drivers are also known to be quite rogue-ish in their behaviour.

by motorcycle taxi

Experience close contact travel.

Do you have a helmet?	你这儿有头盔吗? *nǐ zhè ér yǒu tóu kuī ma*
It's too dangerous!	太危险了! *tài wēi xiǎn le*
Please slow down!	慢点儿! *màn dián ér*
Stop now!	停! *tíng*
Shit! I almost fell down.	妈的，差点掉下去! *mā de ， chà diǎn diào xià qu*
Give me some discount!	打个折吧! *dǎ gè zhé ba*

In suburban areas and small towns, the motorized bicycle (similar to a moped) and the three-wheeled motor bicycle are popular forms of transportation. They can be as fast as motor cars and some of them operate as 'taxis'. The fares are of course much cheaper, but you'll need to negotiate a price with the driver (who won't speak any English!).

by rickshaws

Take it slow and easy...

How much to go to...?	请问去...多少钱? *qǐng wèn qù ... duō shǎo qián*
That's too expensive!	太贵了! *tài guì le*
Can it be cheaper?	便宜点? *pián yi diǎn*
Please ride slowly.	请慢一点! *qǐng màn yì diǎn*
Stop here please!	在这儿停! *zài zhè ér tíng*
Turn (Left/Right)!	(左 / 右) 转! *(zuǒ / yòu) zhuǎn*
Can you stop a while? I want to take a photo here.	可以停一下吗? 我想拍张照片。 *ké yǐ tíng yí xià ma ? wǒ xiǎng pāi zhāng zhào piàn*

by car

Can't give up the luxury of having your own car?

Where can I rent a car?	请问在哪可以租车? *qǐng wèn zài nǎ ké yǐ zū chē*
I'd like to rent ...	我想租... *wǒ xiǎng zū ...*
an automatic.	自动车。 *zì dòng chē*

a car with air conditioning. 一辆带空调的车。
yí liàng dài kōng tiáo de chē

How much does it cost per day / week?	请问租一天 / 一周多少钱? *qǐng wèn zū yì tiān / yì zhōu duō shǎo qián*
Is mileage / insurance included?	包含里程 / 保险在内吗? *bāo hán lǐ chéng / báo xiǎn zài nèi ma*
Where's the next gas station?	请问下一个加油站在哪? *qǐng wèn xià yí gè jiā yóu zhàn zài nǎ*
Is it self-service?	是自助式的吗? *shì zì zhù shì de ma*
Fill it up, please.	请加满。 *qǐng jiā mǎn*

car trouble

Having a breakdown?

My car broke down.	我的车抛锚了。 *wǒ de chē pāo máo le*
Can you send a mechanic / tow truck?	可以派修车师傅 / 拖车来吗? *ké yǐ pài xiū chē shī fu / tuō chē lái ma*
I've run out of gas.	我的车没油了。 *wǒ de chē méi yóu le* Duh!
I have a flat.	我的轮胎漏气了。 *wǒ de lún tāi lòu qì le*
I've locked the keys in the car.	我的钥匙锁在车里了。 *wǒ de yào shi suǒ zài chē lǐ le* Nice one.

auto wreck

If you get pulled over or worse, these expressions may help.

He / She ran into me.	他 / 她撞到我了。 *tā / tā zhuàng dào wǒ le*
He / She was driving <u>too fast</u> / <u>too close</u>.	他 / 她开得<u>太快</u> / <u>太近</u>。 *tā / tā kāi dé <u>tài kuài</u> / <u>tài jìn</u>*
I didn't see the sign.	我没有看见标志。 *wǒ méi yǒu kàn jiàn biāo zhì* Excuses, excuses.

by bike

Calling all bikers.

I'd like to rent …	我想租... *wǒ xiǎng zū …*
a bicycle.	自行车。 *zì xíng chē*
a moped.	助力车。 *zhù lì chē*
a motorbike.	摩托车。 *mó tuō chē*
How much does it cost <u>per day</u> / <u>week</u>?	请问租<u>一天</u> / <u>一周</u>多少钱? *qǐng wèn zū <u>yì tiān</u> / <u>yì zhōu</u> duō shǎo qián* Don't get screwed; confirm the price in advance.

3 MONEY

get cash

Get your RMB and start spending your money!

Where's the nearest bank?	请问最近的银行在哪? *qǐng wèn zuì jìn de yín háng zài nǎ*
Can I exchange foreign currency here?	这里可以兑换外币吗? *zhè lǐ ké yǐ duì huàn wài bì ma*
I'd like to change some dollars / pounds into RMB.	我希望将一些美元 / 英镑兑换成人民币。 *wǒ xī wàng jiāng yì xiē měi yuán / yīng bàng duì huàn chéng rén mín bì*
I want to cash some travelers checks.	我想将一些旅行支票兑换成现金。 *wǒ xiǎng jiāng yì xiē lǚ xíng zhī piào duì huàn chéng xiàn jīn*
What's the exchange rate?	汇率多少? *huì lǜ duō shǎo*

Currency exchange is only available at airports, major banks, hotels and a few major departmental stores. (Hotels only provide this service to house guests.) Take note that not all bank branches provide currency exchange service. And bring along your travel documents as you will need to present them during the transaction. Traveler's checks are not widely accepted, except at most banks.

ATM

Get cash fast.

Where are the ATMs [cash machines]?	请问哪儿有取款机 [ATM]? *qǐng wèn nǎ ér yǒu qǔ kuǎn jī [ATM]*
Can I use my card in the ATM?	我的卡能在取款机 [ATM] 上使用吗? *wǒ de kǎ néng zài qǔ kuǎn jī [ATM] shàng shǐ yòng ma*
The machine has eaten my card.	我的卡被吞了。 *wǒ de kǎ bèi tūn le*

charge it

Can't figure out the currency exchange? Avoid the hassle and use your credit card.

Can I withdraw money on my credit card here?	这里可以用信用卡提取现金吗? *zhè lǐ ké yǐ yòng xìn yòng kǎ tí qǔ xiàn jīn ma*
Do you take credit cards?	你接受信用卡吗? *nǐ jiē shòu xìn yòng kǎ ma*
I'll pay by credit card.	我用信用卡支付。 *wǒ yòng xìn yòng kǎ zhī fù*

FACT Most international credit cards are accepted in major hotels and departmental stores. (Look for credit card logos displayed at entrances or cashier counters.) Everywhere else – in restaurants, shops, and convenience stores – cash is the primary mode of payment. You may be able to withdraw cash from ATMs using your credit card, but it's best to check this with your bank before heading for China.

pay up

Here's how to part with your hard-earned dough.

How much is it?	多少钱? *duō shǎo qián*
Do you accept travelers checks?	您这里接受旅行支票吗? *nín zhè lǐ jiē shòu lǚ xíng zhī piào ma*
Could I have a receipt please?	请问能给我一张发票吗? *qǐng wèn néng gěi wǒ yì zhāng fā piào ma*

FACT When you make a purchase in China, remember to ask for an official invoice or "fā piào". Sales receipts issued by vendors are not recognized as "official invoice" in China. An official invoice is a formatted document issued by the local authorities to the business establishment and it bears two official stamps – one from the authorities and the other from the vendor. The "fā piào" is the official proof of purchase, and you will need it for any exchanges, refunds, or claims (if anything should go awry with your purchases).

There is no sales tax per se in China. So you don't pay any direct taxes on your purchases, and therefore there is no tax refund for tourists.

HOTEL

get a room

You know you want to.

Can you recommend a hotel in …?	能帮我推荐一间在…的旅馆吗? *néng bāng wǒ tuī jiàn yì jiān zài … de lǚ guǎn ma*
Is it near the center of town?	是在市中心附近吗? *shì zài shì zhōng xīn fù jìn ma* You've gotta be close to the bars and clubs, right?!
How much is it per night?	住一晚多少钱? *zhù yì wǎn duō shǎo qián*
Is there anything cheaper?	有没有更便宜的? *yǒu méi yǒu gèng pián yi de*
Could you reserve me a room there, please?	请帮我在那里定一间房。 *qǐng bāng wǒ zài nà lǐ dìng yì jiān fáng*
I have a reservation.	我有预定。 *wǒ yǒu yù dìng*
My name is …	我是… *wǒ shì …*
I confirmed by e-mail.	我用电子邮件确认过。 *wǒ yòng diàn zǐ yóu jiàn què rèn guò*
Could we have adjoining rooms?	有没有相连的房间? *yǒu méi yǒu xiāng lián de fáng jiān*

at the hotel

Need a room for tonight? Ask the right questions.

Do you have a room?	还有房间吗? *hái yǒu fáng jiān ma*

I'd like … | 我想要…
wǒ xiǎng yào …

a single / double room. | 一个单人间 / 双人间。
yí gè dān rén jiān / shuāng rén jiān

a room with a bath / shower. | 一个带浴缸 / 淋浴的房间。
yí gè dài yù gāng / lín yù de fáng jiān

a non-smoking room | 一间禁止吸烟的房间。
yì jiān jìn zhǐ xī yān de fáng jiān

gotta have

Things you can't do without.

Does the hotel have …? | 这家旅馆有没有…?
zhè jiā lǚ guǎn yǒu méi yǒu …

cable TV	有线电视 *yǒu xiàn diàn shì*
internet access	网络 *wǎng luò*
a restaurant	餐馆 *cān guǎn*
room service	客房服务 *kè fáng fú wù*
a gym	健身房 *jiàn shēn fáng*
a swimming pool	游泳池 *yóu yǒng chí*
a Wi-Fi® area	无线网络 *wú xiàn wǎng luò*

Is there … in the room? 请问房间里有没有…?
qǐng wèn fáng jiān lǐ yǒu méi yǒu …

air conditioning 空调
kōng tiáo

a phone 电话
diàn huà

a TV 电视
diàn shì

price

It all comes down to one thing.

How much is it …? …多少钱?
… duō shǎo qián

per night / week 每晚/每周
měi wǎn / měi zhōu

Does the price include …? 请问这个价格包含…吗?
qǐng wèn zhè ge jià gé bāo hán … ma?

breakfast 早餐
zǎo cān

Do I have to pay a deposit? 必须缴押金吗?
bì xū jiǎo yā jīn ma

problems

Tell 'em what's bothering you.

I've lost my key. 我的钥匙丢了。
wǒ de yào shi diū le

The lock is broken.	锁坏了。 *suǒ huài le*
The … doesn't work.	…坏了。 *… huài le*
fan	风扇 *fēng shàn*
heat	暖气 *nuǎn qì*
light	灯 *dēng*
There's no <u>hot water</u> / <u>toilet paper</u>.	没有<u>热水</u> / <u>卫生纸</u>。 *méi yǒu <u>rè shuǐ</u> / <u>wèi shēng zhǐ</u>*

Don't get burnt out. China uses the 220-volt, 50-cycle AC. If you're bringing your gizmos to China, check to see if you'll need a voltage converter. A variety of electrical outlets can be found in China, so a good all-around adaptor plug set is recommended. The most common outlets are those that fit a two-pin plug with flat blades, or a three-pin plug with oblique flat blades.

necessities

More importantly…

Where's the bar?	请问酒吧在哪? *qǐng wèn jiǔ bā zài nǎ* This may be the most important expression in the entire book.
Where's the swimming pool?	请问游泳池在哪? *qǐng wèn yóu yǒng chí zài nǎ*

Where are the restrooms?	请问洗手间在哪? *qǐng wèn xí shǒu jiān zài nǎ*
What time is the front door locked?	请问前门什么时候关? *qǐng wèn qián mén shén me shí hou guān*
What time is breakfast served?	请问早餐时间是几点? *qǐng wèn zǎo cān shí jiān shì jǐ diǎn* *If breakfast is included, don't miss out!*
Could you wake me at … please?	可以在…点叫醒我吗? *ké yǐ zài … diǎn jiào xǐng wǒ ma*
Can I leave this in the hotel safe?	请问我能将这存放在酒店保险箱吗? *qǐng wèn wǒ néng jiāng zhè cún fàng zài jiǔ diàn báo xiǎn xiāng ma*
May I have an extra …?	能多给我…吗? *néng duō gěi wǒ … ma?*
bath towel	一条浴巾 *yì tiáo yù jīn*
blanket	一张毯 *yì zhāng tǎn*
pillow	一个枕头 *yí gè zhěn tou*
roll of toilet paper	一卷卫生纸 *yì juàn wèi shēng zhǐ*
Are there any messages for me?	有没有人给我留口信? *yǒu méi yǒu rén gěi wǒ liú kǒu xìn* *Waiting for that special someone to call?*

hostel

Looking for budget accommodations? The language you need is right here.

Do you have any places left for tonight?	今晚还有空床位吗? *jīn wǎn hái yǒu kōng chuáng wèi ma*
Do you rent bedding?	请问这里出租寝具吗? *qǐng wèn zhè lǐ chū zū qǐn jù ma*
What time are the doors locked?	请问什么时候关门? *qǐng wèn shén me shí hou guān mén*
I have an International Student Card.	我有一张国际学生证。 *wǒ yǒu yì zhāng guó jì xué sheng zhèng*

homestay

A great alternative to the hostel.

Do you have any rooms for tonight?	请问你这儿今晚有房间吗? *qǐng wèn nǐ zhè ér jīn wǎn yǒu fáng jiān ma*
How much for one night?	多少钱一晚? *duō shǎo qián yì wǎn*
Do you have a package rate?	住宿时间长，有优惠吗? *zhù sù shí jiān cháng , yǒu yōu huì ma*
Does the room come with an attached bathroom?	我的房间有独立卫生间吗? *wǒ de fáng jiān yǒu dú lì wèi shēng jiān ma*

Is there any public transportation/ a supermarket nearby?	附近有公共交通 / 超市吗? *fù jìn yǒu gōng gòng jiāo tōng / chāo shì ma*
Do you offer dinner/ guided tours?	你们提供晚餐 / 导游服务吗? *nǐ mén tí gōng wǎn cān / dǎo yóu fú wù ma*

the scoop

For cheap accommodation in China, you have a choice of the budget hotels, youth hostels or guest houses. Budget hotels are available in most cities. They are cheap and pretty basic. If you want to give the youth hostels or guest houses a try, do some online research of your own first. Guest houses are generally more common in the more rural areas such as Yunnan and Lijiang.

check out

It's time to go.

What time do we have to check out?	请问什么时候必须退房? *qǐng wèn shén me shí hou bì xū tuì fáng*
May I have my bill, please?	请帮我结帐。 *qǐng bāng wǒ jié zhàng*
I think there's a mistake in this bill.	帐单可能有错误。 *zhàng dān kě néng yǒu cuò wù*
I've taken … from the mini-bar.	我从迷你吧台拿了…。 *wǒ cóng mí nǐ bā tái ná le …* You lush.

5 FOOD

where to eat

What are ya in the mood for?

Let's go to …	我们一起去…吧 *wǒ men yì qǐ qù … ba*
a buffet.	吃自助餐。 *chī zì zhù cān*
a cafe.	咖啡厅。 *kā fēi tīng*
a cafeteria.	餐厅。 *cān tīng*
a fast-food joint. (McDonald's, KFC, Pizza Hut)	快餐店。 （麦当劳，肯德基，必胜客） *kuài cān diàn* *(mài dāng láo , kěn dé jī ,* *bì shèng kè)*
a restaurant.	餐馆。 *cān guǎn*
a little eating place.	小吃店。 *xiǎo chī diàn*
a steam pot restaurant.	火锅店。 *huǒ guō diàn*
a dumpling restaurant.	饺子馆。 *jiǎo zi guǎn*
Yonghe King.	永和大王。 *yǒng hé dà wang* A popular Chinese-style fast-food restaurent. Think noodles, dumplings, soya drinks, etc.

yo! Now that you know where to eat, you'd better learn when to eat.

Breakfast

Grab breakfast anytime between 7–10 a.m. There's a variety of Chinese style breakfast offerings to choose from: steamed stuffed-buns, soya bean milk, you-tiao, porridge, etc. Get these from the local eateries and markets where they are the cheapest and most authentic. Otherwise, there's the ever-dependable continental breakfast that is served in most hotels.

Lunch

Lunch is early: from 11a.m.–2 p.m. For most Chinese, lunch is a quick and simple affair. You can savour fuss-free Chinese food at local food courts, kiosks or local restaurants. (It used to be the norm to take an afternoon siesta after lunch!)

Dinner

The Chinese have dinner between 6–9 p.m. The pace for dinner is usually much slower. It is almost like a reward after a hard day's work. Dinner is also more elaborate and usually lasts much longer then breakfast or lunch. Most Chinese will indulge in a drink or two during dinner.

Chinese meals generally consist of meat, and vegetable dishes, soup, rice and drinks. The number of dishes ordered depends on the number of people dining together. For example, 10-12 dishes will usually be ordered for a group of 10. If you have dinner by yourself or with only one or two friends, you may like to order something simpler like a bowl of noodles for each person.

fast food

In a rush? Grab a quick bite so you can keep sightseeing…

Is there a … restaurant nearby? 请问附近有没有...餐馆?
qǐng wèn fù jìn yǒu méi yǒu … cān guǎn

cheap 便宜的
pián yi de

Chinese 中
zhōng

vegetarian 素食
sù shí

Where can I find …? 请问在哪儿可以找到...?
qǐng wèn zài nǎ ér ké yǐ zhǎo dào …

a burger stand 汉堡店
hàn bǎo diàn

a café 咖啡厅
kā fēi tīng

a fast-food joint 快餐店
kuài cān diàn

a pizzeria 匹萨店
pǐ sà diàn

I'd like …	我想要… *wǒ xiǎng yào …*
a burger.	一个汉堡。 *yí gè hàn bǎo*
fries.	一份薯条。 *yí fèn shǔ tiáo*
a pizza.	一个匹萨。 *yí gè pǐ sà*
a sandwich.	一份三明治。 *yí fèn sān míng zhì*
It's to go.	带走。 *dài zǒu*
That's all, thanks.	就这些，谢谢。 *jiù zhè xiē , xiè xiè*
Enjoy your meal!	请慢用! *qǐng màn yòng*

street fest

Cheap and good food.

What's this? / What do you call this?	这是什么 / 这叫什么? *zhè shì shén me / zhè jiào shén me*
How much is one serving?	多少钱一份? *duō shǎo qián yí fèn*
Is it spicy?	辣不辣? *là bu là*
Give me one serving to try.	给我一份尝尝。 *gěi wǒ yí fèn cháng cháng*

How do you eat this? Can you show me?	应该怎么吃？可以教我吗？ *yīng gāi zěn me chī ? ké yǐ jiāo wǒ ma*
Can you give me a bag to put this in?	可以给我一个袋子吗？ *ké yǐ gěi wǒ yí gè dài zi ma*

table manner

Go ahead, treat yourself. You deserve a meal at a swanky resaurant!

A table for two, please.	两人桌，谢谢。 *liǎng rén zhuō , xiè xiè*
Could we sit ...?	我们能不能坐在...? *wǒ men néng bu néng zuò zài ...?* Find a cozy, romantic spot.
outside	外面 *wài miàn*
in a non-smoking area	无烟区 *wú yān qū*
by the window	靠窗的地方 *kào chuāng de dì fang*
Where are the restrooms?	请问洗手间在哪? *qǐng wèn xí shǒu jiān zài nǎ*
Waiter! / Waitress!	服务员！ *fú wù yuán*
Could you tell me what this is?	请问这是什么? *qǐng wèn zhè shì shén me* Avoid the shock when your meal arrives...

What's in it?	里面是什么? *lǐ miàn shì shén me*
Without …	不要... *bú yào …* *Just tell them the ingredient you hate!*
May I have some …?	可以给我一些...? *ké yǐ gěi wǒ yì xiē …*
I can't eat food containing …	我不吃有...的食物 *wǒ bù chī yǒu … de shí wù* *Just fill in the blank with what bothers you.*
Do you have vegetarian meals?	请问提供素食餐吗? *qǐng wèn tí gōng sù shí cān ma*
I'm a vegan.	我吃素食。 *wǒ chī sù shí*

complaints

Go ahead and make a big stink.

That's not what I ordered.	这不是我点的。 *zhè bú shì wǒ diǎn de*
I asked for …	我点的是... *wǒ diǎn de shì*
The food is cold.	这菜是冷的。 *zhè cài shì lěng de*
This isn't clean.	这不干净。 *zhè bù gān jìng*
How much longer will our food be?	还有多久才上菜? *hái yǒu duō jiǔ cái shàng cài* *You must be famished!*

We can't wait any longer. We're leaving.	我们不能再等了。我们要走了。 *wǒ men bù néng zài děng le .* *wǒ men yào zǒu le*
We have been waiting for a long time.	我们已经等了很长时间。 *wǒ men yǐ jīng děng le hěn cháng shí jiān*
We have a bus to catch. Can you do our order first?	我们要赶巴士。可以先上我们的菜吗? *wǒ men yào gǎn bā shì* *ké yǐ xiān shàng wǒ men de cài ma*

good or gross?

Give the chef a compliment—or not.

It's …	这… *zhè …*
delicious.	味道很好。 *wèi dào hěn hǎo*
disgusting.	很难吃。 *ěn nán chī*
It's …	这… *zhè …*
foul.	真恶心。 *zhēn ě xīn*
(super) good.	味道很棒。 *wèi dào hěn bàng*
gross.	真倒胃口。 *zhēn dǎo wèi kǒu*
vile.	难吃死了。 *nán chī sǐ le*

This dish tastes great.	这道菜味道太好了。 *zhè dào cài wèi dào tài hǎo le*
You are a great cook.	你真是个好厨师。 *nǐ zhēn shì gè hǎo chú shī*
Sorry, I'm not used to the taste.	对不起，我不太习惯这个味道。 *duì bù qǐ , wǒ bú tài xí guàn zhè ge wèi dào*
It has a rather unique taste.	它的味道很独特。 *tā de wèi dào hěn dú tè*

pay up

How much did that meal set you back?

The check, please.	结帐，谢谢。 *jié zhàng , xiè xie*
We'd like to pay separately.	我们各付各的。 *wǒ men gè fù gè de* Goin' Dutch?
It's all together, please.	一起付，谢谢。 *yì qǐ fù , xiè xie*
I think there's a mistake in this check.	帐单可能有错误。 *zhàng dān kě néng yǒu cuò wù*
What is this amount for?	这怎么算的? *zhè zěn me suàn de*
I didn't have that. I had …	我没有点这个。 我点的是... *wǒ méi yóu diǎn zhè ge . wǒ diǎn de shì …*
Is service included?	请问包括服务费了吗? *qǐng wèn bāo kuò fú wù fèi le ma* Sometimes it is, sometimes it isn't—always best to ask.

Can I pay with this credit card?	我能不能用信用卡支付? *wǒ néng bu néng yòng xìn yòng kǎ zhī fù*
I've forgotten my wallet.	我钱包忘带了。 *wǒ qián bāo wàng dài le* *Oh, god!*
I don't have enough money.	我的钱不够。 *wǒ de qián bú gòu* *Pretty embarrassing…*
Could I have a receipt?	可以给我发票吗? *ké yǐ gěi wǒ fā piào ma*

breakfast

Whether you have it early or late, ask for…

I'd like (some) …	我想要（一些）… *wǒ xiǎng yào (yì xiē) …*
bread.	面包。 *miàn bāo*
butter.	黄油。 *huáng yóu*
eggs.	鸡蛋。 *jī dàn*
jam.	果酱。 *guǒ jiàng*
juice.	果汁。 *guǒ zhī*
milk.	牛奶。 *niú nǎi*
rolls.	面包卷。 *miàn bāo juǎn*
toast.	烤面包。 *kǎo miàn bāo*

soup's on

Homemade and delicious—here are the top picks.

Soup with fish, shrimp and pork balls	三鲜汤 *sān xiān tāng*
Hot pickled vegetable soup with shredded pork	榨菜肉丝汤 *zhà cài ròu sī tāng*
Egg soup with tomatoes	西红柿鸡蛋汤 *xī hóng shì jī dàn tāng*
Fish head and tofu soup	鱼头豆腐汤 *yú tóu dòu fu tāng*
Pork ribs and soy bean soup	排骨黄豆汤 *pái gǔ huáng dòu tāng*

seafood

You've gotta try the fish and seafood!

Hot and spicy crayfish	麻辣小龙虾 *má là xiǎo lóng xiā*
Liquor-soaked crabs	醉蟹 *zuì xiè*
Steamed fish head with diced hot red peppers	剁椒鱼头 *duò jiāo yú tóu*
West lake fish in vinegar gravy	西湖醋鱼 *xī hú cù yú*
Sautéed hardshell crab with rice cake	毛蟹炒年糕 *máo xiè chǎo nián gāo*

you carnivore

A meat-eater's dream come true. Here are the must-haves.

I'd like some … 我想要（一些）…
wǒ xiǎng yào (yì xiē) …

bacon. 熏肉。
xūn ròu

beef. 牛肉。
niú ròu

chicken. 鸡肉。
jī ròu

ham. 火腿。
huó tuǐ

lamb. 羊肉。
yáng ròu

pork. 猪肉。
zhū ròu

sausage. 香肠。
xiāng cháng

steak. 牛排。
niú pái

veal. 小牛肉。
xiǎo niú ròu

Stewed minced pork in savoury suace 红烧狮子头
hóng shāo shī zi tóu

Braised pork 东坡肘子
dōng pō zhǒu zi

Mao's stewed pork 毛氏红烧肉
máo shì hóng shāo ròu
Chairman Mao's favorite dish.

Minced beef steamed with flour 粉蒸肉
fěn zhēng ròu

the scoop

Chinese cuisine can be broadly divided into eight different regional varieties. And among them, there are probably thousands of colorful dishes worth trying. (Every different style of cuisine can be found in any major city.) These are just a few examples.

Sichuan cuisine 川菜 *(chuān cài)*
Spicy beancurd 麻婆豆腐 (má pó dòu fu)
Spicy diced chicken 宫保鸡丁 (gōng bǎo jī dīng)
Shredded pork with fish suace 鱼香肉丝 (yú xiāng ròu sī)
Translucent sliced beef 灯影牛肉 (dēng yǐng niú ròu)

Guangdong cuisine 粤菜 *(yuè cài)*
Roasted suckling pig 烤乳猪 (kǎo rǔ zhū)
Steamed turtle 清蒸甲鱼 (qīng zhēng jiǎ yú)
Snake with sliced bamboo shoot 笋片烧蛇 (sǔn piàn shāo shé)

Shandong cuisine 鲁菜 *(lǔ cài)*
Grilled chicken 德州扒鸡 (dé zhōu pá jī)
Bird's nest soup 清汤燕窝羹 (qīng tāng yàn wō gēng)
Fried clams 油爆大蛤 (yóu bào dà há)
Lotus flower and shrimp 荷花大虾 (hé huā dà xiā)

Fujian cuisine 闽菜 *(mǐn cài)*
Steamed chicken meatball with egg-white
芙蓉鸡丸 (fú róng jī wán)
Fried prawn shaped as a pair of fish 油炸对虾 (yóu zhà duì xiā)
Crisp pomfret (fish) with litchi 荔枝鲳鱼 (lì zhī chāng yú)

the scoop

Huaiyang cuisine 淮阳菜 *(huái yáng cài)*
Yincai vegetables with sliced chicken
蔬菜炒鸡片 (shū cài chǎo jī piàn)
Crab meat and minced pork casserole
砂锅蟹肉丸 (shā guō xiè ròu wán)
Chicken broth with corn
奶油鸡丝玉米汤 (nǎi yóu jī sī yù mǐ tāng)
Squid with crispy rice 鱿鱼锅巴 (yóu yú guō bā)

Zhengjiang cuisine 浙菜 *(zhè cài)*
Braised pork 东坡肘子 (dōng pō zhǒu zi)
West lake fish in vinegar gravy 西湖醋鱼 (xī hú cù yú)
Shrimp with "dragon-well" tea leaves
龙井虾肉 (lóng jǐng xiā ròu)
"Beggar's chicken" (Whole chicken baked in earth)
叫花鸡 (jiào huā jī)

Hunan cuisine 湘菜 *(xiāng cài)*
Dong'an chicken 东安鸡 (dōng ān jī)
Braised dried pork with eel slices 红烧肉 (hóng shāo ròu)
Spring chicken with cayenne pepper 辣子鸡丁 (là zi jī dīng)

Anhui cuisine 徽菜 *(huī cài)*
Huangshan stewed pigeon 黄山醉鸽 (huáng shān zuì gē)
Gourd duck 葫芦鸭 (hú lu yā)
Crisp pork with pine nuts 松仁排骨 (sōng rén pái gǔ)

local cuisine

Oriental flavor at its best ...

Beijing roast duck	北京烤鸭 *běi jīng kǎo yā*
Pork lungs in chili sauce	夫妻肺片 *fū qī fèi piàn* *This literally means "sliced husband-and-wife's lungs"! No wonder Chinese restaurant menus get so much bad press.*
Sauteed shredded pork with pepper & garlic sauce	鱼香肉丝 *yú xiāng ròu sī*
Poached pork in spicy sauce	水煮肉片 *shuǐ zhǔ ròu piàn*
Spicy chicken cubes	宫保鸡丁 *gōng bǎo jī dīng*
Sweet and sour spareribs	糖醋排骨 *táng cù pái gǔ*
Fried egg with tomato	西红柿炒鸡蛋 *xī hóng shì chǎo jī dàn*
Shredded potato with green peppers	青椒土豆丝 *qīng jiāo tǔ dòu sī*

herbivore

For something a little lighter, try these favorites.

Mapo (hot and spicy) beancurd	麻婆豆腐 *má pó dòu fu*

Stir-fried cabbage with vinegar sauce	醋溜白菜 *cù liū bái cài*
Sauteed string bean	干煸四季豆 *gān biān sì jì dòu*
Broccoli with oyster sauce	蚝油芥兰 *háo yóu jiè lán*

Your basic veggies...

carrots	胡萝卜 *hú luó bo*
cucumber	黄瓜 *huáng guā*
green beans	青豆 *qīng dòu*
lettuce	莴苣 *wō jù*
mushrooms	香菇 *xiāng gū*
onions	洋葱 *yáng cōng*
peas	豌豆 *wān dòu*
potatoes	土豆 *tǔ dòu*
tomatoes	西红柿 *xī hóng shì*

dessert

End your meal with any one of these delicious sweets.

Stewed milk beancurd	双皮奶 *shuāng pí nǎi*
Herbal jelly	龟苓膏 *guī líng gāo*
Egg tart	蛋挞 *dàn tà*
Rice balls in fermented glutinous rice syrup	醪糟汤圆 *láo zāo tāng yuán* Probably an acquired taste.

overeating

Did you just pig out?

I'm full.	我吃饱了。 *wǒ chī bǎo le*
I ate too much.	我吃多了。 *wǒ chī duō le*
I'm overstuffed.	我吃撑了。 *wǒ chī chēng le*

6 DRINKS

what to drink

When you need to detox, ask for…

I'd like a …	我想要… *wǒ xiǎng yào …*
(hot) chocolate.	（热）巧克力饮料。 *(rè) qiǎo kè lì yǐn liào*
coke.	可乐。 *kě lè*
juice.	果汁。 *guǒ zhī*
apple-	苹果 *píng guǒ*
grapefruit-	柚子 *yòu zi*
orange-	桔子 *jú zǐ*
mineral water.	矿泉水。 *kuàng quán shuǐ*

the scoop

Despite the rest of the world's obsession with coffee and coffee culture, tea remains the most popular beverage in China. The Chinese started drinking tea way before the 6th century and that's probably why tea has become highly entrenched in the lives of the Chinese people. The five main types of tea sold in China are: green tea, black tea, wulong tea, compressed tea and scented tea.

Life can get a little rough for coffee addicts in China. Most of the time, coffee, especially 'real' coffee and not instant granular or powderized versions, can be extremely hard to find outside the big cities and hotels. You have been warned!

The Chinese drink tea like water. Everywhere you go – in restaurants, hotels, people's homes and offices – tea is served; even if you haven't asked for it! If you really loathe tea, fret not, bottled water, juices and soft drinks are always available; you've just got to ask for it.

beer

Ready for a buzz?

Do you have … beer?	请问有没有...啤酒? *qǐng wèn yǒu méi yǒu … pí jiǔ ?*
bottled	瓶装 *píng zhuāng*
draft	生 *shēng*
A … beer, please.	请来一瓶...啤酒。 *qǐng lái yì píng … pí jiǔ .*
light	淡 *dàn*
dark	黑 *hēi*

the scoop

If you want to sample some local brews, check out brands such as Tsingtao, China Blue Ribbon, Yanjing, Sie-Tang Lio and Zhujiang. Local beers sold in convenience stores and supermarkets are reasonably priced (about 3-8 RMB for a 500ml bottle) but expect to pay more if you are drinking at clubs or bars.

FACT Tipping is not a must but it is generally appreciated. Usually, tipping is done in more upscale places like hotels and restaurants. You're not expected to tip at roadside eateries, smaller restaurants or convenience stores.

drink up

There's no faster way to get a party started.

Do you want ...?	你想要...吗? *nǐ xiǎng yào ... ma ?*
an aperitif	开胃酒 *kāi wèi jiǔ*
wine	酒 *jiǔ*

a glass of red wine	一杯红酒 *yì bēi hóng jiǔ*
a shot	一个 shot *yí gè shot*
a gin and tonic	金汤尼 *jīn tāng ní*
a screwdriver	一杯 screwdriver *yì bēi screwdriver*

FACT The Chinese like their drinks. Meals are washed down with drinks. Celebrations are rarely done without any drinking. Businesses are conducted over drinks. Unhappiness and sorrow are washed away with drinks. Scores can even be settled through drinking sessions!

If you want to raise a toast like a Chinese person, just hold up your drink, clink glasses together, and say "gān bēi" (or "cheers"). Bear in mind though that "gān bēi" literally means "emptying the cup" so use it sparingly.

wine

Go ahead and order a glass—or bottle—of the best.

May I see the wine list, please?	我能看一下酒水单吗? *wǒ néng kàn yí xià jiǔ shuǐ dān ma*

Can you recommend a wine?	你能帮我们推荐一种葡萄酒? *nǐ néng bāng wǒ men tuī jiàn yì zhǒng pú tao jiǔ*
I'd like …	我想要… *wǒ xiǎng yào …*
a bottle of …	一瓶 *yì píng*
a carafe of …	一壶 *yī hú*
a glass of …	一杯 *yì bēi*

FACT The Chinese word for liquor is "jiǔ". Chinese liquor can be quite high in alcohol content, so look out before you take a sip. There are two kinds of liquor – bái jiǔ (white 'wine'), like máo tái (茅台), and wǔ liáng yè (五粮液); and huáng jiǔ (yellow 'wine'), like nǚ ér hóng (女儿红).

Make friends at a bar.

– 能请你喝一杯吗?
néng qǐng nǐ hē yì bēi ma
Can I buy you a drink?

– 当然。
dāng rán
Sure, why not.

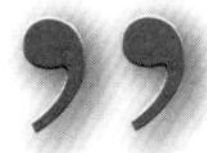

cheers

Before you drink, make a toast.

Let's celebrate!	来庆祝一下吧！ *lái qìng zhù yí xià ba*
Let's cheer!	我们来干杯吧！ *wǒ men lái gān bēi ba*
Cheers!	干杯！ *gān bēi*

hangover

Drank too much? Not feeling too well?

I like to drink.	我喜欢喝酒。 *wǒ xǐ huan hē jiǔ*
I'm tipsy!	我喝醉了！ *wǒ hē zuì le*
I've had one drink too many.	我喝得太多了。 *wǒ hē dé tài duō le*
I'm hung over.	我喝多了头痛。 *wǒ hē duō le tóu tòng*

HAVIN' FUN

beach bum

Grab your shades and get some sun.

Is it a nude beach?	这个是天体海滩吗? *zhè ge shì tiān tǐ hǎi tān ma*
Is there a swimming pool here?	这里有游泳池吗? *zhè lǐ yǒu yóu yǒng chí ma*
Is it safe to swim / dive here?	在这游泳 / 跳水安全吗? *zài zhè yóu yǒng / tiào shuǐ ān quán ma*
Is there a lifeguard?	这里有没有救生员? *zhè lǐ yǒu méi yǒu jiù shēng yuán* What you really want to know is: Is the lifeguard hot?!
I want to rent ...	我想租... *wǒ xiǎng zū ...*
a deck chair.	轻便折叠躺椅。 *qīng biàn zhé dié táng yǐ*
a jet ski.	水上摩 托 。 *shuǐ shàng mó tuō*
a motorboat.	摩托艇。 *mó tuō tǐng*
a surfboard.	冲浪板。 *chōng làng bǎn*
an umbrella.	遮阳伞。 *zhē yáng sǎn*
waterskis.	滑水用具。 *huá shuǐ yòng jù*

Most people don't usually associate China with beaches but... with a coastline that stretches more than 18,000 km, China has dozens of beautiful beaches to offer. From Qingdao to Hainan, beaches scattered along the western coast of China are a haven for sun seekers. Sanya in Hainan island has even been touted as the Hawaii of Asia.

party time

Let the Chinese show you how to have a good time.

What's there to do at night?	请问这里晚上有什么活动? *qǐng wèn zhè lǐ wǎn shang yǒu shén me huó dòng*
Let's hang out tonight.	今晚我们一起去玩吧。 *jīn wǎn wǒ men yì qǐ qù wán ba*
Let's go to ...	我们一起去... *wǒ men yì qǐ qù ...*
the movies.	看电影。 *kàn diàn yǐng*
the theater.	看戏。 *kàn xì*
a concert.	听音乐会。 *tīng yīn yuè huì*

Can you recommend a ...?	你能不能推荐一个...? *nǐ néng bu néng tuī jiàn yí gè ...*
Is there ... in town?	城里有...吗? *chéng lǐ yǒu ... ma*
a bar	酒吧 *jiǔ bā*
a dance club	舞厅 *wǔ tīng*
a gay club	同志俱乐部 *tóng zhì jù lè bù*
a nightclub	夜总会 *yè zǒng huì*
What type of music do they play?	请问他们放什么样的音乐? *qǐng wèn tā men fàng shén me yàng de yīn yuè*
How do I get there?	请问怎么去那里? *qǐng wèn zěn me qù nà lǐ*

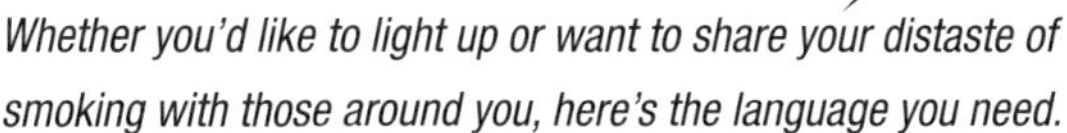

smoke

Whether you'd like to light up or want to share your distaste of smoking with those around you, here's the language you need.

Do you smoke?	你抽烟吗? *nǐ chōu yān ma*
Want to have a smoke?	想抽烟吗? *xiǎng chōu yān ma*
Do you have a cigarette?	你这儿有烟吗? *nǐ zhè ér yǒu yān ma*

the scoop

You'll find few smoke-free areas in China. Smoking is generally allowed and accepted in most public places. Although some restaurants have smoking and non-smoking sections, the smoking restriction is not always enforced in the non-smoking section.

spa

You need complete relaxation.

I'd like ...	我想要… *wǒ xiǎng yào ...*
a facial.	做脸。 *zuò liǎn*
a manicure.	美甲。 *měi jiǎ*
a massage.	按摩。 *àn mó*
a pedicure.	修脚。 *xiū jiǎo*
a bikini wax.	比基尼蜜蜡脱毛。 *bǐ jī ní mì là tuō máo*
an eyebrow wax.	蜡脱眉毛。 *là tuō méi mao*

the sights

Now that you're looking good, see and be seen.

Where's the tourist information office?	请问旅游信息服务台在哪? *qǐng wèn lǚ yóu xìn xī fú wù tái zài nǎ*
Can you recommend a sightseeing tour?	你能帮我推荐一个旅行团吗? *nǐ néng bāng wǒ tuī jiàn yí gè lǚ xíng tuán ma* *A great way to meet other cute travelers, like yourself!*
Are there any trips to ...?	这儿有去...的旅行团? *zhè ér yǒu qù ... de lǚ xíng tuán*
What time does the tour start?	旅行团什么时候出发? *lǚ xíng tuán shén me shí hou chū fā*
How much does the tour cost?	旅行团多少钱? *lǚ xíng tuán duō shǎo qián*
What time do we get back?	什么时候回来? *shén me shí hou huí lái*
Is there an English-speaking guide?	有英语导游吗? *yǒu yīng yǔ dǎo yóu ma*
Can we stop here ...?	我们能停一下...吗? *wǒ men néng tíng yí xià ... ma*
to buy souvenirs	买纪念品 *mǎi jì niàn pǐn*
to use the restrooms	去一趟洗手间 *qù yí tàng xí shǒu jiān*
to take photographs	拍照 *pāi zhào* *Capture the memory.*

Would you take a photo of us?	你可以帮我们拍张照吗? *nǐ ké yǐ kě bāng wǒ men pāi zhāng zhào ma* Ask a cute Chinese guy or girl!
Where is ...?	请问...在哪? *qǐng wèn ... zài nǎ*
the art gallery	艺术长廊 *yì shù cháng láng*
the church	教堂 *jiào táng*
the downtown area	市区 *shì qū*
the market	市场 *shì chǎng*
the (war) memorial	（战争）纪念馆 *(zhàn zhēng) jì niàn guǎn*
the museum	博物馆 *bó wù guǎn*
the old town	老城区 *lǎo chéng qū*
the palace	故宫 *gù gōng*
the shopping area	购物区 *gòu wù qū*
How much is the entrance fee?	请问门票多少钱? *qǐng wèn mén piào duō shǎo qián*
Are there any discounts for students?	请问这里出售学生票吗? *qǐng wèn zhè lǐ chū shòu xué sheng piào ma*

the scoop

Did you see something totally cool? Here are the top ten ways to say it.

Wonderful	太棒了 *tài bàng le*
Cool	很酷 *hěn kù*
Awesome	太厉害了 *tài lì hai le*
Great	太牛了 *tài niú le*
Very good	很不错 *hěn bú cuò*
Super cool	超级厉害 *chāo jí lì hai*
Awesome	太强了 *tài qiáng le*
Super!	牛！ /鸟！ / 强！ *niú ! / diǎo ! / qiáng !*
Awesome!	爽！ *shuǎng !*
@&%*# good!	太鸟了！ *tài diǎo le !*

entertainment

In the mood for a little culture?

Do you have a program of events?	你有节目表吗? *nǐ yǒu jié mù biǎo ma*
Can you recommend a good …?	有没有精彩的…可以推荐给我的? *yǒu méi yǒu jīng cǎi de … ké yǐ tuī jiàn gěi wǒ de*
concert	音乐会 *yīn yuè huì*
movie	电影 *diàn yǐng*
When does it start?	什么时候开始? *shén me shí hou kāi shǐ*
Where can I get tickets?	请问售票处在哪儿? *qǐng wèn shòu piào chù zài nǎ ér*
How much are the seats?	请问票多少钱? *qǐng wèn piào duō shǎo qián*
Do you have anything cheaper?	有更便宜的票吗? *yǒu gèng pián yi de piào ma*
Can I have a program?	能给我一份节目表吗? *néng gěi wǒ yí fèn jié mù biǎo ma*

movies

Behind-the-scenes movie lingo…

My favorite movies are …	我最喜欢…。 *wǒ zuì xǐ huan…*

comedies. | 喜剧片。 *xǐ jù piàn*

dramas. | 剧情片。 *jù qíng piàn*

foreign films. | 外国片。 *wài guó piàn*

thrillers. | 惊悚片。 *jīng sǒng piàn*

psycho-thrillers. | 心理惊悚片。 *xīn lǐ jīng sǒng piàn*

What's playing at the movies? | 电影院正在上映什么电影? *diàn yǐng yuàn zhèng zài shàng yìng shén me diàn yǐng*

Is the movie dubbed / subtitled? | 这部电影有配音 / 字幕吗? *zhè bù diàn yǐng yǒu pèi yīn / zì mù ma*

music

Get into the groove.

Do you like ...? | 你喜欢...吗? *nǐ xǐ huan ... ma ?*

dance music | 舞曲 *wú qǔ*

hip-hop | hip-hop

house (music) | house（音乐） *house (yīn yuè)*

jazz | 爵士乐 *jué shì yuè*

pop (music)	流行（音乐） *liú xíng (yīn yuè)*
rap	说唱 *shuō chàng*
reggae	雷鬼 *léi guǐ*
rock and roll	摇滚 *yáo gǔn*
techno	techno
I really like …	我非常喜欢… *wǒ fēi cháng xǐ huan …*
country.	乡村音乐。 *xiāng cūn yīn yuè*
folk.	民乐。 *mín yuè*
soul.	灵魂乐。 *líng hún lè*
Which band is playing?	请问哪支乐队正在表演? *qǐng wèn nǎ zhī yuè duì zhèng zài biáo yǎn*
Are they popular?	他们流行吗? *tā men liú xíng ma*

yo! Can't live without your tunes? Make sure you have these.

a CD player — CD 播放器 *bō fàng qì*

a discman — 随身听 *suí shēn tīng*

an MP3 player — MP 三播放器 *MP sān bō fàng qì*

an iPod™ — iPod™

earphones — 耳机 *ěr jī*

a stereo — 立体声 *lì tǐ shēng*

yo! Here are some traditional festivals in China:

Spring Festival (or Lunar New Year). Usually occurs between mid January to Febuary. Most people take a 7-day break from work to celebrate the beginning of the new year.

Qing Ming Festival (April 4th, or 5th or 6th). The Chinese commemorate their ancestors and relatives who have passed on. It also signals the arrival of spring, and a change in the seasons.

Duan Wu Festival (around June 1st). People eat zòng zǐ (rice wrapped and cooked in leaves) and take part in dragon boat races to commemorate Qu Yuan, a Chinese poet and patriot.

Chong Yang Festival (in early October). This auspicious day falls on the 9th day of the 9th lunar month. People enjoy cake and chrysanthemum blooms as part of the celebrations. Chong Yang is also Senior Citizen's Day in China.

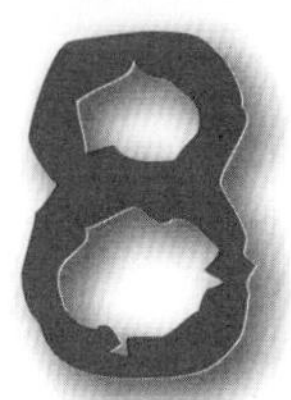

SPORTS

sports

Get active.

Do you want to try ...? 你想不想试试...?
nǐ xiǎng bu xiǎng shì shì ... ?

chi kung 气功
qì gōng

tai chi 太极
tài jí

yoga 瑜伽
yú jiā

I want to... 我想要...
wǒ xiǎng yào ...

cycle. 骑自行车。
qí zì xíng chē

jog. 慢跑。
màn pǎo

rollerblade. 溜旱冰。
liū hàn bīng

ice skate. 去溜冰。
qù liū bīng

surf. 冲浪。
chōng làng

swim. 游泳。
yóu yǒng

Do you want to play ...? 你想不想打...?
nǐ xiǎng bu xiǎng dǎ ... ?

basketball 篮球
lán qiú

tennis	网球 *wǎng qiú*
volleyball	排球 *pái qiú*

I want to ...	我想要... *wǒ xiǎng yào ...*
play pingpong (table tennis)	打乒乓球 *dǎ pīng pāng qiú*
play badminton	打羽毛球 *dǎ yǔ máo qiú*
play football (soccer)	踢足球 *tī zú qiú*

Pingpong or table tennis is one of the most popular sports in China. It is regarded as national sport by the Chinese. Badminton is another favorite sport. The Chinese are also big fans of team sports like football, basketball and volleyball. Some rather interesting traditional sports include rope skipping (跳绳 tiào shén), shuttlecock kicking (踢毽子 tī jiàn zi), and kite flying (放风筝 fàng fēng zheng).

extreme sports

Take your game to the next level.

I want to go …	我想去… *wǒ xiǎng qù …*
skydiving.	跳伞。 *tiào sǎn*
kayaking.	划独木舟。 *huá dú mù zhōu*
mountain-climbing.	登山。 *dēng shān*
rafting.	激流泛舟。 *jī liú fàn zhōu*
bungee jumping.	蹦极。 *bèng jí*

spectator sports

Prefer watching sports to actually playing them?

Is there a soccer game this week?	这个星期有没有足球赛? *zhè ge xīng qī yǒu méi yǒu zú qiú sài*
Which teams are playing?	哪些球队比赛? *nǎ xiē qiú duì bǐ sài*
Can you get me a ticket?	你能帮我买张票吗? *nǐ néng bāng wǒ mǎi zhāng piào ma*
What's the admission charge?	入场票价多少? *rù chǎng piào jià duō shǎo*

soccer match

Show that you're true sports fans by screaming these.

Go!	快! *kuài !*
Let's go!	上! *shàng !*
Get them!	干死丫的! *gān sǐ yā de !*
Goal!	球进了! *qiú jìn le !*
We're the champions!	我们赢了! *wǒ men yíng le !*

insults

Don't forget that harassing the referee and the opponent, it is part of you job as a spectator.

The referee took a bribe!	裁判滚蛋! *cái pàn gǔn dàn !*
Kick him out!	下课! *xià kè !* Literally: Class dismissed!
So predictable!	太假了! *tài jiǎ le !*
You suck!	烂! *làn !* Literally: Rotten.

He sucks!	这个傻逼! *zhè ge shă bī !*
@#&! this player!	操! 这个傻逼! *cào ! zhè ge shă bī !*
Moron!	傻逼! *shă bī !*
@#%* !	操! / 靠! *cào ! / kào !*
Son of a bitch!	婊子养的! *biăo zi yăng de !* Caution: Downright nasty. Use it at your own expense.
Get @#%&* by a dog!	狗日的! *gŏu rì de !* Warning: Super offensive. Be prepared for trouble.

training

Don't let your body go just because you're on vacation.

Can I use ...?	我可以用...吗? *wŏ ké yĭ yòng ... ma ?*
the fitness bike	健身车 *jiàn shēn chē*
the rowing machine	划艇器 *huá tĭng qì*
the treadmill	跑步机 *păo bù jī*
I feel great.	我很好。 *wŏ hén hăo*

I'm in shape.	我身体很健康。 *wǒ shēn tǐ hěn jiàn kāng*
I'm dead tired.	我累死了。 *wǒ lèi sǐ le*
I can't take it anymore.	我不行了。 *wǒ bù xíng le*
I'm sick of it.	我玩腻了。 *wǒ wán nì le*

Gambling is legally prohibited in China – unless you are in Macau. Known as the Monte Carlo of the Orient, Macau is where the Chinese tourists head for some legal gambling thrills and spills. There, you can bet on casino games, horse races, greyhound races, sports, and lotteries.

9 MAKIN' FRIENDS

small talk

Get a conversation goin'.

My name is … 我叫…
wǒ jiào …
A simple way to introduce yourself.

What's your name? 你贵姓?
nǐ guì xìng

Where are you from? 你从哪儿来?
nǐ cóng nǎ ér lái

Whom are you with? 你跟谁一起来的吗?
nǐ gēn shuí yì qǐ lái de ma

I'm on my own. 我自己一个人。
wǒ zì jǐ yí gè rén

I'm with a friend. 我和一个朋友来。
wǒ hé yí gè péng you lái
Oh, really?!

I'm with my … 我和我的…来
wǒ hé wǒ de … lái

- boyfriend / girlfriend. 男朋友 / 女朋友。 *nán péng you / nǚ péng you*
- family. 家人。 *jiā rén*
- parents. 父母。 *fù mǔ*
- father / mother. 爸/妈。 *bà / mā*
- elder brother / sister. 哥哥 / 姐姐。 *gē ge / jiě jie*
- younger brother / sister. 弟弟 / 妹妹。 *dì di / mèi mei*

chitchat

These will help you keep his or her attention.

What do you do?	你做什么的? *nǐ zuò shén me de*
What are you studying?	你学什么的? *nǐ xué shén me de*

I'm studying ...	我主修... *wǒ zhǔ xiū ...*
the arts.	艺术。 *yì shù*
business.	商务。 *shāng wù*
engineering.	工程。 *gōng chéng*
sales.	销售。 *xiāo shòu*
science.	科学。 *kē xué*

Whom do you work for?	你在哪儿上班? *nǐ zài nǎ ér shàng bān*
I work for …	我在…上班 *wǒ zài … shàng bān*
What are your interests?	你对什么感兴趣? *nǐ duì shén me gǎn xìng qù*
What are your hobbies?	你有什么爱好吗? *nǐ yǒu shén me ài hào ma*

makin' plans

Get together.

Are you free tonight?	今晚有空吗? *jīn wǎn yǒu kōng ma*
Can you come for a drink this evening?	今晚能来喝一杯吗? *jīn wǎn néng lái hē yì bēi ma*
Would you like to …?	你想…吗? *nǐ xiǎng … ma*
go dancing	去跳舞 *qù tiào wǔ*
go out to eat	去吃东西 *qù chī dōng xi*
go for a walk	去散步 *qù sàn bù*
Can I bring a friend?	我能带一个朋友吗? *wǒ néng dài yí gè péng you ma*
Where should we meet?	我们在哪儿见面? *wǒ men zài nǎ ér jiàn miàn*

hangin' out

Get a little closer with these.

Let me buy you a drink.	我请你喝一杯。 *wǒ qǐng nǐ hē yì bēi*
What are you going to have?	你想喝什么? *nǐ xiǎng hē shén me*
Why are you laughing?	你笑什么? *nǐ xiào shén me*
Is my Mandarin that bad?	我的普通话有这么差吗? *wǒ de pǔ tōng huà yǒu zhè me chà ma*
Should we go somewhere quieter?	我们是不是应该去更安静的地方? *wǒ men shì bu shì yīng gāi qù gèng ān jìng de dì fang* Such as...?
Thanks for the evening.	今晚很开心，谢谢你! *jīn wǎn hěn kāi xīn，xiè xiè nǐ*

If you are a guy and you invite a girl on a date, you'll probably be expected to pay the bill for the girl. The Chinese are generally quite conservative, and may turn down a date with someone they've just met for the first time.

get a date

Looking to score? Try these.

Hi, how are you?	嗨，你好！ *hēi , nǐ hǎo* *It's simple—but a good way to break the ice.*
Hello, I don't think we've met.	嘿，我们没见过吧。 *hēi , wǒ men méi jiàn guò ba* *If it's is your first visit to China, it's certainly the truth!*
Would you like to sit down?	你想坐下吗？ *nǐ xiǎng zuò xià ma* *This works wonders in a bar or on the subway.*
You are really sexy.	你真的很性感。 *nǐ zhēn de hěn xìng gǎn* *The perfect informal come-on to use in a bar or club.*
Are you a model?	你是模特吗？ *nǐ shì mó tè ma* *You'd be surprised how well this one works.*
You look great!	你真漂亮！ *nǐ zhēn piào liang*
Do you mind if I sit here?	你介意我坐这吗？ *nǐ jiè yì wǒ zuò zhè ma*
You are very pretty / handsome.	你真美 / 帅。 *nǐ zhēn měi / shuài*

You have beautiful eyes.	你的眼睛真漂亮。 *nǐ de yǎn jing zhēn piào liang*
Do you have a boyfriend / girlfriend?	你有男朋友 / 女朋友吗? *nǐ yǒu nán péng you / nǚ péng you ma*
Can I be your friend?	我可以跟你交个朋友吗? *wǒ ké yǐ gēn nǐ jiāo gè péng you ma*
Can I be your boyfriend / girlfriend?	我可以做你的男朋友 / 女朋友吗? *wǒ ké yǐ zuò nǐ de nán péng you / nǚ péng you ma*
Do you believe in love at first sight?	你相信一见钟情吗? *nǐ xiāng xìn yí jiàn zhōng qíng ma*
I am serious about you.	我对你是认真的。 *wǒ duì nǐ shì rèn zhēn de*

refusals

Not your type? Here are the best ways to reject someone.

Thanks, but I'm expecting someone.	谢谢，但我正在等人。 *xiè xiè , dàn wǒ zhèng zài děng rén* Whether this is true or not, he or she will get the hint.
Leave me alone, please.	别烦我! *bié fán wǒ*
Get the heck out of here!	走开! *zǒu kāi*
Go away!	滚开! *gǔn kāi* It's brutal, but effective.
You are not my type.	你不是我的菜。 *nǐ bú shì wǒ de cài*

gay?

Looking for some alternative fun?

Are you gay?	你是同志吗? *nǐ shì tóng zhì ma*
Do you like men / women?	你喜欢男人/女人啊? *nǐ xǐ huan nán rén / nǚ rén ā*
Let's go to a gay bar.	一起去同志酒吧。 *yì qǐ qù tóng zhì jiǔ bā*
He's gay.	他是同志! *tā shì tóng zhì*
She's a lesbian.	她是女同志! *tā shì nǚ tóng zhì*
Get out of the closet!	别瞒了! *bié mán le*

dating

Found a Chinese lover? Here's how to tell your love story.

I made out with him.	我跟他亲热过。 *wǒ gēn tā qīn rè guò*
I'm going out with her.	我跟她在趴拖。 *wǒ gēn tā zài pā tuō*
I french-kissed him.	我跟他舌吻过。 *wǒ gēn tā shé wěn guò*
We got naked.	我们发生过关系。 *wǒ men fā shēng guò guān xi*

sex

A variety of ways to state the obvious…

We …	我们… *wǒ men …*
slept together.	发生关系了。 *fā shēng guān xi le*
made love.	做过爱。 *zuò guò ài*
@#&!ed.	干过。 *gān guò*

safe sex

Protection is a must, in any language.

I use …	我用… *wǒ yòng …*
condoms.	避孕套。 *bì yùn tào*
the pill.	避孕药。 *bì yùn yào*
a diaphragm.	避孕帽。 *bì yùn mào*
Have you been tested for HIV?	你做过 HIV 检查吗? *nǐ zuò guò HIV jiǎn chá ma*
Do you have a condom?	你有避孕套吗? *nǐ yǒu bì yùn tào ma*
Are you using contraceptives?	你在避孕吗? *nǐ zài bì yùn ma*

break up

The best way to end .

It's over between us.	我们之间完了。 *wǒ men zhī jiān wán liǎo* *Be firm!*
Let's just be friends.	让我们做普通朋友吧。 *ràng wǒ men zuò pǔ tōng péng you ba* *Say this only if you mean it.*
I'm breaking up with you.	我们分手吧。 *wǒ men fēn shǒu ba* *End of story...*

closure

Did he or she dump you? Here are the nastiest things you can call your ex.

You're a scumbag.	你真卑劣。 *nǐ zhēn bēi liè*
He is a …	他… *tā …*
pathetic guy.	真可悲。 *zhēn kě bēi*
loser.	是个垃圾。 *shì gè lā jī*

She is a … 她是个… *tā shì gè …*

slut. 贱货。 *jiàn huò*

bitch. 贱人。 *jiàn rén*

10 SHOPPING

where to shop

Grab your wallet and go!

Are we going shopping?	我们是去购物吗? *wǒ men shì qù gòu wù ma*
Do you want to go window shopping?	你是否打算只看不买? *nǐ shì fǒu dǎ suan zhǐ kàn bù mǎi*
Where's the main mall?	请问最大的几个商场在哪儿? *qǐng wèn zuì dà de jǐ gè shāng chǎng zài nǎ ér*
I'm looking for …	我在找... *wǒ zài zhǎo …*
a boutique.	精品店。 *jīng pǐn diàn*
a department store.	百货商店。 *bǎi huò shāng diàn*
a flea market.	跳蚤市场。 *tiào zao shì chǎng*
a market.	市场。 *shì chǎng*
an outlet store.	畅货店。 *chàng huò diàn*
a second-hand store.	二手货商店。 *èr shǒu huò shāng diàn*
a vintage shop.	古董店。 *gú dǒng diàn*
When does the … open / close?	请问...什么时候开门 / 关门? *qǐng wèn … shén me shí hou kāi mén / guān mén*

Where's …?	请问…在哪儿? *qǐng wèn … zài nǎ ér*
the bookstore	书店 *shū diàn*
the camera shop	相机店 *xiàng jī diàn*
the health food store	健康食品商店 *jiàn kāng shí pǐn shāng diàn*
the jewelry store	珠宝店 *zhū bǎo diàn*
the liquor store	酒类专买店 *jiǔ lèi zhuān mǎi diàn*
the market	市场 *shì chǎng*
the music store	音乐商店 *yīn yuè shāng diàn*
the newsstand	报摊 *bào tān*
the pharmacy	药店 *yào diàn*
the shoe store	鞋店 *xié diàn*
the souvenir store	纪念品商店 *jì niàn pǐn shāng diàn*
the sports store	体育用品商店 *tǐ yù yòng pǐn shāng diàn*
Where can I find …?	请问哪儿有…? *qǐng wèn nǎ ér yǒu … ?*
antiques	古董 *gú dǒng*

cheap and trendy women's wear/ men's wear? | 便宜和时尚的女装/男装? *pián yi hé shí shàng de nǚ zhuāng / nán zhuāng*

handicraft | 手工艺品 *shǒu gōng yì pǐn*

a night market | 夜市 *yè shì*

a street market | 市集 *shì jí*

yo! Don't miss Nanjing Road, Huaihai Road, Middle Tibet Road in Shanghai; and Wangfujing, and the Xidan Commercial Street in Beijing. You'll find a mixture of top luxury brands as well as local products in these areas.

customer service

Ask the right questions.

Where's ...? | 请问...在哪儿? *qǐng wèn ... zài nǎ ér ?*

the escalator | 电梯 *diàn tī*

the store map | 商店地图 *shāng diàn dì tú*

Where's ...? | 请问...在哪儿? *qǐng wèn ... zài nǎ ér ?*

customer service | 客户服务 *kè hù fú wù*

the fitting room | 更衣室 *gēng yī shì*

the lingerie department | 女士内衣部 *nǚ shì nèi yī bù*

the men's department | 男士用品部 *nán shì yòng pǐn bù*

the perfume / cosmetics department | 香水 / 化妆品部 *xiāng shuǐ / huà zhuāng pǐn bù*

the register | 出纳处 *chū nà chù*

the shoe department | 鞋部 *xié bù*

the women's department | 女士用品部 *nǚ shì yòng pǐn bù*

Where can I find ...? | 在哪可找到...儿? *zài nǎ kě zhǎo dào ... ér ?*

boot-cut pants | 靴型裤 *xuē xíng kù*

jeans | 牛仔裤 *niú zǎi kù*

a leather jacket | 皮夹克 *pí jiā kè*

low-rise pants | 低腰裤 *dī yāo kù*

a miniskirt | 超短裙 *chāo duǎn qún*

a polo shirt | 球衣 *qiú yī*

I'm looking for … 我正在找…
wǒ zhèng zài zhǎo …

a backpack. 背包。
bèi bāo

books / magazines. 书 / 杂志。
shū / zá zhì

CDs / DVDs. CD / DVD

sales help

Here's how to ask that cute salesperson for assistance.

Can you help me? 你能不能帮我一下?
nǐ néng bu néng bāng wǒ yí xià

Can I try this on? 可以试穿吗?
ké yǐ shì chuān ma

Where's the fitting room? 请问更衣室在哪儿?
qǐng wèn gēng yī shì zài nǎ ér

Could you show me …? 能让我看看…吗?
néng ràng wǒ kàn kan … ma

I'd like to buy … 我想买…
wǒ xiǎng mǎi …

yo! You may want to fill in the blank above with any of these items.

baseball cap	棒球帽 *bàng qiú mào*
bikini	比基尼 *bǐ jī ní*
bra	胸罩 *xiōng zhào*
briefs	内裤 *nèi kù*
boxers	平角短裤 *píng jiǎo duǎn kù*
coat	外套 *wài tào*
denim jacket	牛仔夹克 *niú zǎi jiá kè*
dress	长裙 *cháng qún*
halter top, tank top	女式三角背心、紧身短背心 *nǚ shì sān jiǎo bèi xīn 、 jǐn shēn duǎn bèi xīn*
jeans	牛仔裤 *niú zǎi kù*
messenger bag	斜背包 *xié bèi bāo*
shirt	衬衣 *chèn yī*
shoes	鞋子 *xié zǐ*
day shoes	工作鞋 *gōng zuò xié*

shorts	短裤 *duǎn kù*
skirt	裙子 *qún zi*
socks	短袜 *duǎn wà*
sunglasses	太阳镜 *tài yáng jìng*
swim trunks	游泳裤 *yóu yǒng kù*
thong	丁字裤 *dīng zì kù*
tight T-shirt	紧身体恤 *jǐn shēn tǐ xù*

yo! Looking for something in a particular color? Ask for it in…

beige	米色 *mǐ sè*	orange	桔色 *jú sè*
black	黑色 *hēi sè*	pink	粉红色 *fěn hóng sè*
blue	蓝色 *lán sè*	purple	紫色 *zǐ sè*
brown	褐色 *hè sè*	red	红色 *hóng sè*
gray	灰色 *huī sè*	white	白色 *bái sè*
green	绿色 *lǜ sè*	yellow	黄色 *huáng sè*

Shopping in China can be a thrill because of the attractive bargains, but if you're not happy with your purchases, few stores will give you your money back. You should be able to make an exchange if there is a flaw or defect in the product. Just make sure you have the official invoice or "fā piào" from the vendor.

at the register

Looking to part with your hard-earned dough? Here's the lingo you need to make your purchase.

How much?	请问多少钱? *qǐng wèn duō shǎo qián*
Where do I pay?	请问在哪付钱? *qǐng wèn zài nǎ fù qián*
Do you accept travelers checks?	请问你这里接受旅行支票吗? *qǐng wèn nǐ zhè lǐ jiē shòu lǚ xíng zhī piào ma*
Sorry, I don't have enough money.	对不起，我的钱不够。 *duì bù qǐ ， wǒ de qián bú gòu*
Could I have a receipt please?	请给我一张发票。 *qǐng gěi wǒ yì zhāng fā piào*
I think you've given me the wrong change.	我想你找错钱了。 *wǒ xiǎng nǐ zhǎo cuò qián le*

FACT The price you see on the tag is the price you pay. There are no additional taxes on your purchases. You don't usually have to tip as well (a service tax is already included in the total bill in most upscale restaurants and entertainment venues).

bargains

Put your negotiating skills to use.

Is this on sale?	打折吗? *dǎ zhé ma*
That's too expensive.	太贵了。 *tài guì le*
It's pricey.	很贵。 *hěn guì*
Will you lower the price?	可以便宜点吗? *ké yǐ pián yi diǎn ma*
Can you give me a discount?	可以给我打个折扣吗? *ké yǐ gěi wǒ dǎ gè zhé kòu ma*
Do you have anything cheaper?	有没有更便宜的? *yǒu méi yǒu gèng pián yi de*
I'll think about it.	我考虑一下。 *wǒ kǎo lǜ yí xià*

the scoop

You must bargain with the vendors in the street shops and the flea markets – because they expect you to do so, and you may end up paying a lot more if you don't bargain. Check out Xiangyang market and Qipu Road Market in Shanghai; and Xiu Shui Street in Beijing.

problems

Is there something wrong with your purchase?

This doesn't work.	这个有问题。 *zhè ge yǒu wèn tí*
Can you exchange this, please?	请换一下，谢谢。 *qǐng huàn yí xià , xiè xiè*
I'd like a refund.	我想退货。 *wǒ xiǎng tuì huò*
Here's the receipt.	这是发票。 *zhè shì fā piào*
I don't have the receipt.	我没有发票。 *wǒ méi yǒu fā piào*

at the drugstore

Not feeling well? Here's some help.

Where's the nearest (all-night) pharmacy?	请问最近的（24 小时）药店在哪儿? *qǐng wèn zuì jìn de (ér shí sì xiǎo shí) yào diàn zài nǎ ér*

Can you fill this prescription for me?	可以给我开个处方吗? *ké yǐ gěi wǒ kāi gè chǔ fāng ma*
How much should I take?	请问一次服用多少? *qǐng wèn yí cì fú yòng duō shǎo*
How often should I take it?	请问多久服用一次? *qǐng wèn duō jiǔ fú yòng yí cì*
Are there any side effects?	请问有没有副作用? *qǐng wèn yǒu méi yǒu fù zuò yòng*
What would you recommend for ...?	如果...，你建议吃什么药? *rú guǒ ... ， nǐ jiàn yì chī shén me yào*
a cold	感冒 *gǎn mào*
a cough	咳嗽 *ké sou*
diarrhea	腹泻 *fù xiè*
a hangover	宿醉头痛 *sù zuì tóu tòng*
hay fever	花粉热 *huā fěn rè*
insect bites	蚊虫叮咬 *wén chóng dīng yǎo*
a sore throat	喉咙痛 *hóu lóng tòng*
sunburn	晒伤 *shài shāng*
motion sickness	晕动症 *yūn dòng zhèng*
an upset stomach	反胃 *fǎn wèi*

Can I get it without a prescription? 如果没有处方，我可以购买这些药吗?
rú guǒ méi yǒu chǔ fāng , wǒ ké yǐ gòu mǎi zhè xiē yào ma

Can I have …? 我想买...?
wǒ xiǎng mǎi … ?

antiseptic cream 杀菌霜
shā jūn shuāng

aspirin 阿司匹林
ā sī pǐ lín

bandages 绷带
bēng dài

condoms 避孕套
bì yùn tào

bug repellent 驱蚊剂
qū wén jì

painkillers 止痛药
zhǐ tòng yào

vitamins 维生素
wéi shēng sù

toiletries

Forgot to pack something?

I'd like … 我想要...
wǒ xiǎng yào …

aftershave.  须后水。
xū hòu shuǐ

conditioner.  护发素。
hù fā sù

deodorant.  除臭剂。 *chú chòu jì*

moisturizing cream.  保湿霜。 *bǎo shī shuāng*

razor blades.  剃须刀。 *tì xū dāo*

sanitary napkins.    卫生巾。 *wèi shēng jīn*

shampoo.  洗发水。 *xǐ fā shuǐ*

soap.  肥皂。 *féi zào*

sun block.  防晒霜。 *fáng shài shuāng*

suntan lotion. 晒黑露。 *shài hēi lù*

tampons.   卫生棉。 *wèi shēng mián*

tissues.  手纸巾。 *shóu zhǐ jīn*

toilet paper.   卫生纸。 *wèi shēng zhǐ*

toothpaste. 牙膏。 *yá gāo*

make-up

Ladies, get all dolled up.

I need some … 我需要一些… *wǒ xū yào yì xiē …*

blush. 腮红。 *sāi hóng*

eyeliner.	眼线笔。 *yǎn xiàn bǐ*
eye shadow.	眼影。 *yǎn yǐng*
foundation.	粉底。 *fěn dǐ*
lipgloss / lipstick.	唇彩 / 唇膏。 *chún cǎi / chún gāo*
mascara.	睫毛膏。 *jié máo gāo*
powder.	散粉。 *sàn fěn*

camera shop

Admit it, you're a tourist. You'll need these.

I'm looking for a disposable camera.	我在找一次性相机。 *wǒ zài zhǎo yí cì xìng xiàng jī*
Do you sell … for digital cameras?	请问你这里卖数码相机…吗？ *qǐng wèn nǐ zhè lǐ mài shù mǎ xiàng jī … ma ?*
memory cards	内存卡 *nèi cún kǎ*
batteries	电池 *diàn chí*
When will the photos be ready?	请问这些照片什么时候能好？ *qǐng wèn zhè xiē zhào piàn shén me shí hou néng hǎo*

Most shops open between 8am - 10pm, Mondays to Sundays. Business hours for shopping malls are usually 10am to 10pm every day. There are a growing number of convenience stores that open 24-hours.

11 TECH TALK

internet café

Stay in touch with friends and family at home.

Is there an internet café near here?	请问附近有没有网吧? *qǐng wèn fù jìn yǒu méi yǒu wǎng bā*
Can I access the internet here?	请问这里能上网吗? *qǐng wèn zhè lǐ néng shàng wǎng ma*
What are the charges per hour?	每小时多少钱? *měi xiǎo shí duō shǎo qián*
How do I log on?	怎么登录? *zěn me dēng lù*
I'd like to send a message by e-mail.	我想发电子邮件。 *wǒ xiǎng fā diàn zǐ yóu jiàn*
What's your e-mail address?	你的电子邮件地址是什么? *nǐ de diàn zǐ yóu jiàn dì zhǐ shì shén me*
Check out ...	看看... *kàn kan ...*
this cool computer.	这款很酷的电脑。 *zhè kuǎn hěn kù de diàn nǎo*
this cool laptop.	这款很酷的笔记本电脑。 *zhè kuǎn hěn kù de bǐ jì běn diàn nǎo*
this cool mouse.	这款很酷的鼠标。 *zhè kuǎn hěn kù de shǔ biāo*
Turn it on.	开机。 *kāi jī*
Click here!	单击这里! *dān jī zhè lǐ*

I'm going to …	我想要… *wǒ xiǎng yào …*
go online.	上网。 *shàng wǎng*
send an e-mail.	发电子邮件。 *fā diàn zǐ yóu jiàn*
You need to logout / reboot.	你需要注销 / 重启。 *nǐ xū yào zhù xiāo / chóng qǐ*
My computer crashed.	死机了。 *sǐ jī le*

yo! With over 200 million internet users, China has the second largest Netizen community in the world after the US. It's no surprise then that internet cafes can be found everywhere – from the big cities to the small counties. Prices can be as low as 2-5 RMB per hour. Some places even offer refreshments to help make your internet experience as enjoyable as possible. You'll need to bring along your travel documents as Chinese regulations require internet users to present their IDs to enter an internet Cafe.

laptop

Brought your own laptop? You might need these questions.

Does this hotel / café have Wi-Fi®?	这家酒店 / 咖啡屋有无线网络吗? *zhè jiā jiǔ diàn / kā fēi wū yǒu wú xiàn wǎng luò ma*

Where is the closest hotspot?
最近的无线热点在哪儿?
zuì jìn de wú xiàn rè diǎn zài nǎ ér

Is there a connection fee?
收取连接费吗?
shōu qǔ lián jiē fèi ma

Do I have to register?
我需要注册吗?
wǒ xū yào zhù cè ma

What's your favorite …
你最喜爱的…是什么?
nǐ zuì xǐ ài de … shì shén me

- chatroom
  聊天室
  liáo tiān shì
- webpage
  网页
  wǎng yè
- website
  网站
  lwǎng zhàn

Can you …
你可以…吗?
nǐ ké yǐ … ma ?

- IM someone
  跟我网上聊天
  gēn wǒ wǎng shàng liáo tiān
- send me an e-mail
  给我发电子邮件
  gěi wǒ fā diàn zǐ yóu jiàn
- scroll <u>up</u> / <u>down</u>
  向<u>上</u> / <u>下</u>滚动窗口
  xiàng <u>shàng</u> / <u>xià</u> gǔn dòng chuāng kǒu

phone call

From public to private, the language you need to make a call.

I'd like a phonecard.	我想要一张电话卡。 *wǒ xiǎng yào yì zhāng diàn huà kǎ*
I need to make a phone call.	我需要打个电话。 *wǒ xū yào dǎ gè diàn huà*
Can I ...?	我能不能...? *wǒ néng bu néng ... ?*
get your number	知道你的号码 *zhī dào nǐ de hào mǎ*
call you	给你打电话 *gěi nǐ dǎ diàn huà*
make a call	打个电话 *dǎ gè diàn huà*
I'll give you a call.	我会给你电话。 *wǒ huì gěi nǐ diàn huà*
Here's my number.	这是我的号码。 *zhè shì wǒ de hào mǎ*
Call me.	电话联系! *diàn huà lián xì*
Where's the nearest phone booth?	请问最近的电话亭在哪? *qǐng wèn zuì jìn de diàn huà tíng zài nǎ*
May I use your phone?	我可以用一下你的电话吗? *wǒ ké yǐ yòng yí xià nǐ de diàn huà ma*
It's an emergency.	这很紧急。 *zhè hěn jǐn jí*

What's the number for Information?	请问信息服务台号码是多少? *qǐng wèn xìn xī fú wù tái hào mǎ shì duō shǎo*
I'd like to call collect.	我想拨打对方付费的电话。 *wǒ xiǎng bō dǎ duì fāng fù fèi de diàn huà*
Hello?	喂? *wèi* Say this when you answer the phone.
Yes.	是。 *shì*
It's …	我是... *wǒ shì …* Just add your name.
It's me!	是我! *shì wǒ*
Could I speak with …?	能帮我叫一下...? *néng bāng wǒ jiào yí xià*
I'd like to speak to …	我找... *wǒ zhǎo* A little less uptight than the entry above.
Can I leave a message?	可以留个言吗? *ké yǐ liú gè yán ma* Hope he or she calls you back.
Hold on, please.	请等一下。 *qǐng děng yí xià*

When will he / she be back?	他 / 她什么时候回来? *tā / tā shén me shí hou huí lái* *You're desperate to talk to him or her, huh?*
Will you tell him / her that I called?	你能不能告诉他 / 她我来过电话? *nǐ néng bu néng gào su tā / tā wǒ lái guò diàn huà* *Is he or she avoiding you?*

bye!

End that phone conversation with class.

I'll be in touch.	保持联系。 *bǎo chí lián xì*
Good-bye.	再见。 *zài jiàn*
Gotta go.	走了! *zǒu le* *You're in a rush to get off the phone!*
Later.	回见。 *huí jiàn*
Love you.	爱你。 *ài nǐ*
Let's talk later.	以后再聊。 *yǐ hòu zài liáo*

Public phones are still fairly common in China. There are coin phones and card phones. You can purchase prepaid phone cards from convenience stores. In some rural areas, you may find regular phones doubling up as public phones in front of some shops. You'll have to pay cash to the store owners for the use of the phone.

There are a variety of prepaid phones cards issued by different companies and it is a good idea to compare prices to find the phone card that you need. For instance, some cards offer better discounts for long distance calls.

China uses the standard GSM wireless service that is common throughout Europe and most of Asia. To use your cell phone or mobile phone in China, you'll need a handset that is compatible with this GSM standard. If you are in doubt, you may want to consider renting a phone before leaving for your trip. (Some of these rented sets come with China SIM cards, so you're ready to start making phone calls the moment you land.) You could also purchase a China SIM card at your destination; if you have a handset that works. This is usually a cheaper option to international auto-roam service, but of course it involves more hassle, and you'll have a new China number for your phone.

snail mail

Mail your stuff.

Where is the post office?	邮局在哪? *yóu jú zài nǎ* *Ask a cutie—he or she might even take you there personally.*
What time does the post office open / close?	邮局什么时候开门 / 关门? *yóu jú shén me shí hou kāi mén / guān mén*

A stamp for this postcard, please.	买张明信片的邮票，谢谢。 *mǎi zhāng míng xìn piàn de yóu piào , xiè xiè*
What's the postage for a letter to …?	寄到...需要多少钱? *jì dào … xū yào duō shǎo qián*
I want to send this package …	我想要寄...包裹。 *wǒ xiǎng yào ... jì bāo guǒ*
by airmail.	航空。 *háng kōng*
by express mail.	快递。 *kuài dì*

DICTIONARY
Chinese ➤ English

A

ā sī pǐ lín aspirin
ài love
ài to love
ài hào hobby
àn mó massage
ān quán (wēi xiǎn) safe (dangerous)
ATM (qǔ kuǎn jī) ATM (cash machine)

B

bà bà father
bā shì bus
bái cài cabbage
bǎi huò shāng diàn department store
bái sè white
bāng máng to help
bāo guǒ package
bào jǐng to report (to police)
bāo kuò included
bǎo shī moisturizing
bào tān newsstand
báo xiǎn insurance
báo xiǎn xiāng safe
bēi cup
bēi glass
bèi bāo backpack
bēi liè scumbag
bèi tōu le stolen
bēng dài bandage
bèng jí bungee jumping
bǐ jī ní bikini
bǐ jī ní mì là tuō máo bikini wax
bì yùn mào diaphragm
bì yùn tào condom
biāo zhì sign
bó wù guǎn museum
bú no
bù department (in store)
bú yào without

C

cái pàn referee
cān guǎn restaurant
can yin meal
CD bō fàng qì CD player
cè suǒ bathroom
chá tea
cháng long
cháng láng gallery
chāo shì supermarket
chē car
chē fèi fare (transport)
chèn yī shirt
chī to eat
chī sù vegan
chóng fù to repeat
chōng làng to surf
chōng làng bǎn surfboard
chōu yān to smoke
chú chòu jì deodorant
chǔ fāng prescription
chū nà chù register (payment)
chuáng bed
chuāng window

chún lips
chún cǎi lip gloss
chún gāo lipstick
cuò / chà bad
cuò wù mistake

D

dǎ diàn huà to phone
dǎ zhé on sale
dǎ zhé sale
dài / dài zi bag
dān chéng one-way (ticket)
dǎn gù chún cholesterol
dān rén jiān single room
dǎo yóu fú wù guided tour
děng to wait
dēng light (in building)
dēng jī mén gate (at airport)
dēng lù to log on (computer)
dēng shān mountain-climbing
dī dǎn gù chún low-cholesterol
dī nà de low-sodium
dī rè liàng low-calorie
dì tiě subway
dì zhǐ address
dī zhī fáng low-fat
diàn shop
diàn store
diàn chí battery
diàn huà phone
diàn huà telephone
diàn huà kǎ telephone card
diàn huà tíng phone booth
diàn nǎo computer
diàn shì television
diàn shì television set
diàn yǐng movie
diàn zǐ yóu jiàn dì zhǐ e-mail address
dìng to order
dìng to reserve
dīng zì kù thong
diū le lost
dòu bean
dú mù zhōu kayak
duǎn kù shorts
duǎn wà socks
duì huàn to cash (a check)
duō jiǔ how long (time)
duō shǎo cost
duō shǎo how many
duō shǎo qián how much

E

ěr jī earphones
èr shì sì xiǎo shí yào diàn all-night pharmacy

F

fā piào receipt
fǎn wèi upset stomach
fān yì to translate
fáng jiān room
fáng shài shuāng sun block
féi zào soap
fěn dǐ foundation (make-up)
fěn hóng sè pink
fēng shàn fan
fù to pay (money)

fù mǔ parents
fū rén ma'am
fú wù service
fú wù tái information desk
fù xiè diarrhea

G

gān dry
gān jìng clean
gǎn mào cold (flu)
gāo tǎ tower
gē ge / dì di brother
gēng yī shì fitting room
gōng jī attack
gòu wù qū shopping area
gù gōng palace
guān to close
guì expensive
guó jì xué sheng zhèng International Student Card
guǒ jiàng jam
guǒ zhī juice

H

hài hi
hǎi tān beach
háng bān flight
háng kōng airmail
háo oyster
hǎo good
hē to drink
hè sè brown
hēi dark
hēi sè black
hóng sè red
hóu lóng throat
hóu lóng tòng sore throat
hù fā sù conditioner
hú luó bo carrot
hù mǎ xiàng jī digital camera
huá bǎn to skateboard
huā fěn rè hay fever
huá shuǐ yòng jù waterski
huá tǐng qì rowing machine
huà zhuāng pǐn bù cosmetics department
huàn change
huàn to exchange
huáng guā cucumber
huáng sè yellow
huáng yóu butter
huī sè gray
huǒ chē train
huó tuǐ ham

J

jī chǎng airport
jì chéng chē cab
jì chéng chē taxi
jī dàn egg
jì niàn guǎn memorial
jì niàn pǐn souvenir
jī ròu chicken (meat)
jiā kè jacket
jiā mǎn to fill
jiā rén family
jiǎn chá check
jiàn kāng shí pǐn shāng diàn health food store

jiàn shēn chē fitness bike
jiàn yì to recommend
jiào táng church
jiě jie (elder sister) **/ mèi mei** (younger sister) sister
jié mù biǎo program
jié zhàng check (in a restaurant)
jǐn tight
jǐn jí emergency
jīn tāng ní gin and tonic
jīn wǎn tonight
jǐng chá police
jǐng chá jú police station
jiǔ wine
jiǔ bā bar
jiǔ lèi zhuān mǎi diàn liquor store
jiù shēng yuán lifeguard
jú sè orange (color)

K

kǎ card
kā fēi coffee
kā fēi tīng café
kāi open
kāi shǐ to start
kàn to look
kǎo miàn bāo toast
kè fáng fú wù room service
ké sou cough
kē xué science
kōng tiáo air conditioning
kù pants
kuài fast
kuài dì express mail
kuàng quán shuǐ mineral water

L

lán qiú basketball
lán sè blue
lǎo chéng qū old town
lèi tired
lěng cold
lǐ chéng mileage
lì tǐ shēng stereo
lín yù bath
lín yù shower
lǐng shì guǎn consulate
liū hàn bīng to rollerblade
lǘ guǎn hotel
lǜ sè green
lǚ xíng tuán sightseeing tour
lǚ xíng tuán tour
lǚ xíng zhī piào travelers checks
lǚ yóu xìn xī fú wù tái tourist information office

M

mā mother
mǎi to buy
màn pǎo to jog
màn yì diǎn slowly
mào zǐ cap
měi jiǎ manicure
méi mao eyebrow
měi xiǎo shí per hour
méi yǒu fū zhì gluten-free
mén door

mǐ sè beige
miàn bāo bread
miàn bāo juǎn roll (bread)
míng bɑi to understand
míng xìn piàn postcard
mó tuō tǐng motorboat
MP sān bō fàng qì MP3 player

N

nà sodium
ná to take (something)
nán chī awful (taste)
nán péng you boyfriend
nèi cún kǎ memory card
nèi kù briefs
niú nǎi milk
niú pái steak
niú ròu beef
niú zǎi kù jeans
nòng huài damaged
nǚ péng you girlfriend
nǚ tóng zhì (slang) lesbian
nuǎn qì heat (in building)

O

ǒu tù to barf

P

pǎo bù jī treadmill
pèi yīn dubbed
péng you friend
pí jiǔ beer
piào ticket
piào liɑng beautiful
píng bottle
píng guǒ apple
píng jiǎo duǎn kù boxers
pú tɑo jiǔ wine (red /white)

Q

qí zì xíng chē cycling
qián money
qián bāo wallet
qián bì currency
qián bì duì huàn chù currency exchange office
qiáng jiān rape
qiǎng jié mugging
qiǎo kè lì chocolate
qǐn jù bedding
qǐng please
qīng dòu green bean
qiú duì team (sports)
qiú sài ball game / sports game
qǔ kuǎn jī cash machine (ATM)
què rèn to confirm
qún zi skirt

R

rè hot
rè liàng calorie
rè qiǎo kè lì hot chocolate

S

sàn fěn powder
shā jūn shuāng antiseptic cream
shài hēi lù suntan lotion
shài shāng sunburn

shāng chǎng mall
shén me shí hou what time
shén me shí hou when
shēng draft (beer)
shì yes
shì chǎng market
shì gù accident
shí kè biǎo schedule
shì qū downtown
shì qū town
shí wù food
shì zhèng tīng town hall
shǒu hand
shǒu gè the first
shǒu tí xiāng suitcase
shóu zhǐ jīn tissues
shū book
shū diàn bookstore
shǔ tiáo fries
shuāng rén jiān double room
shuǐ water
shuǐ shàng mó tuō jet ski
sù shí vegetarian
sù zuì tóu tòng hangover (slang)
suǒ lock
suǒ to lock

T

tài yáng sun
tài yáng jìng sunglasses
tǎn blanket
táng niào bìng rén diabetic
tí qǔ withdrawal
tǐ xù T-shirt
tì xū dāo razor
tǐ yù yòng pǐn shāng diàn sports store
tiān day
tiān tǐ hǎi tān nude beach
tiào sǎn skydiving
tìao wǔ to dance
tiào zao shì chǎng flea market
tíng to stop
tóng zhì (slang) gay
tōu qiè theft
tǔ dòu potato
tuì huò refund
tuō chē tow truck

W

wài guó foreign
wài miàn outside
wài tào coat
wán play
wǎn night
wǎn cān dinner
wán diǎn delay
wān dòu peas
wǎn shang evening
wǎng bā internet café
wáng fǎn round-trip
wǎng luò internet access
wǎng qiú tennis
wǎng yè webpage
wèi stomach
wèi dào hěn hǎo delicious
wèi shēng jiān toilet
wèi shēng jīn sanitary napkin

wèi shēng mián tampon
wéi shēng sù vitamin
wèi shēng zhǐ toilet paper
wěn kiss
wén chóng insect
wō jù lettuce
wǔ tīng dance club
wú xiàn wǎng luò Wi-Fi® area
wú yān qū non-smoking area

X

xǐ fā shuǐ shampoo
xī hóng shì tomato
xì jù drama
xǐ jù piàn comedy
xí shǒu jiān restroom
xiā shrimp
xià chē to get off (a bus, train, etc.)
xià yí gè next
xiàn line (train / subway)
xiān sheng sir
xiāng cháng sausage
xiāng gū mushroom
xiàng jī camera
xiàng jī diàn camera shop
xiǎo mài bù snack bar
xiǎo niú ròu veal
xiǎo shí hour
xiǎo tōu thief
xié shoe
xiè crab
xiě to write
xìn xī information
xìn yòng kǎ credit card
xìng sex
xíng li baggage / luggage
xiōng zhào bra
xiū chē shī fu mechanic
xiū jiǎo pedicure
xū hòu shuǐ aftershave lotion
xū yào to need
xué sheng student
xūn ròu bacon

Y

yā duck
yá gāo toothpaste
yān cigarette
yǎn jing eye
yǎn yǐng eye shadow
yáng cōng onion
yáng ròu lamb
yào pill
yào diàn drugstore / pharmacy
yào shi key
yè zǒng huì nightclub
yì one
yǐ chair
yí cì xìng xiàng jī disposable camera
yī sheng doctor
yì shù cháng láng art gallery
yì tiān per day
yì zhōu per week
yín háng bank
yīn yuè music
yīn yuè huì concert
yīng shì zú qiú soccer

yīng yǔ English
yóu gas (car)
yòu right (direction)
yóu jú post office
yǒu kōng free (available)
yóu piào stamp (mail)
yóu tài jiāo de jié shí kosher
yóu yǒng to swim
yóu yǒng chí swimming pool
yóu yǒng kù swim trunks
yòu zi grapefruit
yú fish
yù dìng reservation
yù gāng bathtub
yù jīn bath towel
yù jīn towel
yuǎn far
yùn dòng bìng airsickness
yūn dòng zhèng motion sickness

Z

zài nǎ ér where
zǎo cān breakfast
zhà cài pickle
zhàn station (bus, train)
zhàn tái platform
zhàn zhēng jì niàn guǎn war memorial
zhàng dān / jié zhàng bill
zhǎo to speak
zhào piàn photo
zhé kòu discount
zhē yáng sǎn umbrella
zhěn tou pillow
zhī fáng fat
zhǐ tòng yào painkiller
zhí wù yuán botanical garden
zhí wù yuán garden
zhōu week
zhū bǎo jewelry
zhù lì chē moped
zhū ròu pork
zì dòng automatic
zì mù subtitle
zǐ sè purple
zì xíng chē bicycle
zì zhù cān buffet
zú qiú football
zuì hòu the last
zuì jìn nearest / recently
zuì xǐ ài / zuì xǐ huan favorite
zuǒ left (direction)
zuò to take (a mode of transport)
zuò liǎn facial (spa)
zuò wèi seat

DICTIONARY
English ➤ Chinese

A

accident shì gù
address dì zhǐ
aftershave lotion xū hòu shuǐ
air conditioning kōng tiáo
airmail háng kōng
airport jī chǎng
airsickness yùn dòng bìng
all-night pharmacy èr shì sì xiǎo shí yào diàn
antiseptic cream shā jūn shuāng
apple píng guǒ
art gallery yì shù cháng láng
aspirin ā sī pǐ lín
ATM (cash machine) ATM (qǔ kuǎn jī)
attack gōng jī
automatic zì dòng

B

backpack bèi bāo
bacon xūn ròu
bad cuò / chà
bag dài / dài zi
baggage xíng li
bandage bēng dài
bank yín háng
bar jiǔ bā
basketball lán qiú
bath lín yù
bath towel yù jīn
bathroom cè suǒ
bathtub yù gāng
battery diàn chí
beach hǎi tān
bean dòu
beautiful piào liang
bed chuáng
bedding qǐn jù
beef niú ròu
beer pí jiǔ
beige mǐ sè
bicycle zì xíng chē
bikini bǐ jī ní
bikini wax bǐ jī ní mì là tuō máo
bill zhàng dān / jié zhàng
black hēi sè
blanket tǎn
blue lán sè
book shū
bookstore shū diàn
botanical garden zhí wù yuán
bottle píng
boxers píng jiǎo duǎn kù
boyfriend nán péng you
bra xiōng zhào
bread miàn bāo
breakfast zǎo cān
briefs nèi kù
brother gē ge / dì di
brown hè sè
buffet zì zhù cān
bungee jumping bèng jí
bus bā shì
butter huáng yóu

C

cab jì chéng chē
cabbage bái cài
café kā fēi tīng
calorie rè liàng
camera xiàng jī
camera shop xiàng jī diàn
cap mào zǐ
car chē
card kǎ
carrot hú luó bo
cash machine (ATM) qǔ kuǎn jī
CD player CD bō fàng qì
chair yǐ
change huàn
check jiǎn chá
check (in a restaurant) jié zhàng
chicken (meat) jī ròu
chocolate qiǎo kè lì
cholesterol dǎn gù chún
church jiào táng
cigarette yān
clean gān jìng
(night) club yè zǒng huì
coat wài tào
coffee kā fēi
cold lěng
cold (flu) gǎn mào
comedy xǐ jù piàn
computer diàn nǎo
concert yīn yuè huì
conditioner hù fā sù
condom bì yùn tào
consulate lǐng shì guǎn
cosmetics department huà zhuāng pǐn bù
cost duō shǎo
cough ké sou
crab xiè
credit card xìn yòng kǎ
cucumber huáng guā
cup bēi
currency qián bì
currency exchange office qián bì duì huàn chù
cycling qí zì xíng chē

D

damaged nòng huài
dance club wǔ tīng
dark hēi
day tiān
delay wán diǎn
delicious wèi dào hěn hǎo
deodorant chú chòu jì
department (in store) bù
department store bǎi huò shāng diàn
diabetic táng niào bìng rén
diaphragm bì yùn mào
diarrhea fù xiè
digital camera hù mǎ xiàng jī
dinner wǎn cān
discount zhé kòu
disgusting (taste) nán chī
disposable camera yí cì xìng xiàng jī

doctor yī sheng
door mén
double room shuāng rén jiān
downtown shì qū
draft (beer) shēng (pí jǐu)
drama xì jù
drugstore yào diàn
dry gān
dubbed pèi yīn
duck yā

E

earphones ěr jī
egg jī dàn
e-mail address diàn zǐ yóu jiàn dì zhǐ
emergency jǐn jí
English yīng yǔ
evening wǎn shang
expensive guì
express mail kuài dì
eye yǎn jing
eye shadow yǎn yǐng
eyebrow méi mao

F

facial (spa) zuò liǎn
family jiā rén
fan fēng shàn
far yuǎn
fare (transport) chē fèi
fast kuài
fat zhī fáng
father bà bà
favorite zuì xǐ ài / zuì xǐ huan
first shǒu gè **(flight)** / dì yí tàng **(train)**
fish yú
fitness bike jiàn shēn chē
fitting room gēng yī shì
flea market tiào zao shì chǎng
flight háng bān
food shí wù
football zú qiú
foreign wài guó
foundation (make-up) fěn dǐ
free (available) yǒu kōng
friend péng you
fries shǔ tiáo

G

game (sports) qiú sài
gallery cháng láng
garden zhí wù yuán
gas (car) yóu
gate (airport) dēng jī mén
gay tóng zhì (slang)
gin and tonic jīn tāng ní
girlfriend nǚ péng you
glass bēi
gluten-free méi yǒu fū zhì
good hǎo
grapefruit yòu zi
gray huī sè
green lǜ sè
green bean qīng dòu
guided tour dǎo yóu fú wù

H

ham huó tuǐ
hand shǒu
hangover sù zuì tóu tòng
hay fever huā fěn rè
health food store jiàn kāng shí pǐn shāng diàn
heat (in building) nuǎn qì
hi hài
hobby ài hào
hot rè
hot chocolate rè qiǎo kè lì
hotel lǘ guǎn
hour xiǎo shí
how long (time) duō jiǔ
how many duō shǎo
how much duō shǎo qián

I

included bāo kuò
information xìn xī
information desk fú wù tái
insect wén chóng
insurance báo xiǎn
International Student Card guó jì xué sheng zhèng
internet access wǎng luò
internet café wǎng bā

J

jacket jiā kè
jam guǒ jiàng
jeans niú zǎi kù
jet ski shuǐ shàng mó tuō
jewelry zhū bǎo
juice guǒ zhī

K

kayak dú mù zhōu
key yào shi
kiss wěn
kosher yóu tài jiāo de jié shí

L

lamb yáng ròu
last zuì hòu
left (direction) zuǒ
lesbian nǚ tóng zhì (slang)
lettuce wō jù
lifeguard jiù shēng yuán
light (in building) dēng
line (train / subway) xiàn
lip gloss chún cǎi
lips chún
lipstick chún gāo
liquor store jiǔ lèi zhuān mǎi diàn
lock suǒ
long cháng
lost diū le
love ài
low-calorie dī rè liàng
low-cholesterol dī dǎn gù chún
low-fat dī zhī fáng
low-sodium dī nà de
luggage xíng li

M

ma'am fū rén
mall shāng chǎng
manicure měi jiǎ
market shì chǎng
massage àn mó
meal cān yǐn
mechanic xiū chē shī fu
memorial jì niàn guǎn
memory card nèi cún kǎ
mileage lǐ chéng
milk niú nǎi
mineral water kuàng quán shuǐ
mistake cuò wù
moisturizing bǎo shī
money qián
moped zhù lì chē
mother mā
motion sickness yūn dòng zhèng
motorboat mó tuō tǐng
mountain-climbing dēng shān
movie diàn yǐng
MP3 player MP sān bō fàng qì
mugging qiǎng jié
museum bó wù guǎn
mushroom xiāng gū
music yīn yuè

N

near (nearby) fù jìn
newsstand bào tān
next xià yí gè
night wǎn
nightclub yè zǒng huì
no bú
non-smoking area wú yān qū
nude beach tiān tǐ hǎi tān

O

old town lǎo chéng qū
on sale dǎ zhé
one yì
one-way (ticket) dān chéng
onion yáng cōng
open kāi
orange (color) jú sè
outside wài miàn
oyster háo

P

package bāo guǒ
painkiller zhǐ tòng yào
palace gù gōng
pants kù
parent fù mǔ
peas wān dòu
pedicure xiū jiǎo
per day yì tiān
per hour měi xiǎo shí
per week yì zhōu
pharmacy yào diàn
phone diàn huà
phone booth diàn huà tíng
photo zhào piàn
pickle zhà cài
pill yào
pillow zhěn tou
pink fěn hóng sè

platform zhàn tái
play wán
please qǐng
police jǐng chá
police station jǐng chá jú
pork zhū ròu
post office yóu jú
postcard míng xìn piàn
potato tǔ dòu
powder sàn fěn
prescription chǔ fāng
program jié mù biǎo
purple zǐ sè

R

rape qiáng jiān
razor tì xū dāo
receipt fā piào
red hóng sè
referee cái pàn
refund tuì huò
register (payment) chū nà chù
reservation yù dìng
restaurant cān guǎn
restroom xí shǒu jiān
right (direction) yòu
roll (bread) miàn bāo juǎn
room fáng jiān
room service kè fáng fú wù
round-trip wáng fǎn
rowing machine huá tǐng qì

S

safe báo xiǎn xiāng
safe (dangerous) ān quán (wēi xiǎn)
sale dǎ zhé
sanitary napkin wèi shēng jīn
sausage xiāng cháng
schedule shí kè biǎo
science kē xué
scumbag bēi liè
seat zuò wèi
service fú wù
sex xìng
shampoo xǐ fā shuǐ
shirt chèn yī
shoe xié
shop diàn
shopping area gòu wù qū
shorts duǎn kù
shower lín yù
shrimp xiā
sightseeing tour lǚ xíng tuán
sign biāo zhì
single room dān rén jiān
sir xiān sheng
sister jiě jie **(elder sister)** / mèi mei **(younger sister)**
skirt qún zi
skydiving tiào sǎn
slowly màn yì diǎn
snack bar xiǎo mài bù

soap féi zào
soccer yīng shì zú qiú
socks duǎn wà
sodium nà
sore throat hóu lóng tòng
souvenir jì niàn pǐn
sports store tǐ yù yòng pǐn shāng diàn
stamp (mail) yóu piào
station zhàn **(bus,train)** / jú **(police)**
steak niú pái
stereo lì tǐ shēng
stolen bèi tōu le
stomach wèi
store diàn
student xué sheng
subtitle zì mù
subway dì tiě
suitcase shǒu tí xiāng
sun tài yáng
sun block fáng shài shuāng
sunburn shài shāng
sunglasses tài yáng jìng
suntan lotion shài hēi lù
supermarket chāo shì
surfboard chōng làng bǎn
swim trunks yóu yǒng kù
swimming pool yóu yǒng chí

T

tampon wèi shēng mián
taxi jì chéng chē
tea chá
team (sports) qiú duì
telephone diàn huà
telephone card diàn huà kǎ
television diàn shì
television set diàn shì
tennis wǎng qiú
theft tōu qiè
thief xiǎo tōu
thong dīng zì kù
throat hóu lóng
ticket piào
tight jǐn
tired lèi
tissues shóu zhǐ jīn
to barf ǒu tù
to buy mǎi
to cash (a check) duì huàn
to close guān
to confirm què rèn
to dance tìao wǔ
to drink hē
to eat chī
to exchange huàn
to fill jiā mǎn
to get off (a bus, train, etc.) xià chē
to help bāng máng
to jog màn pǎo
to lock suǒ
to log on (computer) dēng lù
to look kàn
to love ài
to need xū yào

to order dìng
to pay (money) fù
to phone dă diàn huà
to recommend jiàn yì
to repeat chóng fù
to report (to police) bào jĭng
to reserve dìng
to rollerblade liū hàn bīng
to skateboard huá băn
to smoke chōu yān
to speak zhăo
to start kāi shĭ
to stop tíng
to surf chōng làng
to swim yóu yŏng
to take ná **(something) /** fú **(medication)**
to take (somewhere) zuò **(transportation) /** dài **(take me to)**
to translate fān yì
to understand míng bɑl
to wait dĕng
to write xiĕ
toast kăo miàn bāo
toilet wèi shēng jiān
toilet paper wèi shēng zhĭ
tomato xī hóng shì
tonight jīn wăn
toothpaste yá gāo
tour lǚ xíng tuán
tourist information office lǚ yóu xìn xī fú wù tái
tow truck tuō chē
towel yù jīn
tower gāo tă
town shì qū
town hall shì zhèng tīng
train huŏ chē
travelers checks lǚ xíng zhī piào
treadmill păo bù jī
T-shirt tĭ xù

U

umbrella zhē yáng săn
upset stomach făn wèi

V

veal xiăo niú ròu
vegan chī sù
vegetarian sù shí
vitamin wéi shēng sù

W

wallet qián bāo
war memorial zhàn zhēng jì niàn guăn
water shuĭ
waterski huá shuĭ yòng jù
webpage wăng yè
week zhōu
what time shén me shí hou
when shén me shí hou
where zài nă ér
white bái sè
Wi-Fi® area wú xiàn wăng luò
window chuāng

wine jiǔ
wine (red /white) pú tao jiǔ
withdrawal tí qǔ
without bú yào

Y

yellow huáng sè
yes shì